Dynamic systems development method

Contents

Trademark notice

The following are trademarks or registered trademarks of their respective companies:

Oracle; SQL PLus; SQL Forms; Oracle 7; PL/SQL and Oracle System 7 are trademarks of Oracle Corporation UK Ltd.

SELECT is a trademark of Select Software Ltd.

NEXTSTEP OO is a trademark of NEXT Corporation.

CENTURA SQL Windows is a trademark of Centura Software Corporation.

Microsoft Word; MIcrosoft Windows; MS Access and Windows 95 are trademarks of Microsoft Corporation.

Systemator is a trademark of Sysdeco Group.

Micro Focus COBOL is a trademark of Micro Focus.

Unix is a trademark of X/Open Company Ltd.

Informix is a trademark of Informix Software Inc.

One Per Desk and DRS 3000 are trademarks of International Computers Ltd (ICL).

Rapid Application Development (RAD) is a trademark of James Martin.

Preface

The pressure from businesses to deliver software support in ever-decreasing time-scales has led to the development and publication of the Dynamic Systems Development Method (DSDM) by a growing, UK-based Consortium of organisations. The Consortium members include organisations with internal IT departments (such as British Airways in the UK and Freddie Mac in the United States) and IT-based companies of varying sizes, from giants, such as IBM and Oracle, down to small consultancy practices.

DSDM provides a framework of controls and best practice for the rapid application development (RAD) of high-quality business system solutions. The method has achieved considerable success and has become the *de facto* standard for RAD in the UK. The UK successes have led to international expansion in the use of the method.

Many organisations have moved to using DSDM and many more are considering doing so. The detail of the method is defined and described in the *DSDM Manual* published by the Consortium, but at the time of writing there is no book on the market that provides practical guidance on the use of the method or one that provides case studies from real DSDM projects. The DSDM Consortium has decided to keep the *DSDM Manual* short, and it should be used as a reference document rather than a guide to the implementation and application of DSDM. This book provides an overview of the method and covers the main areas of concern. It does not replace the *Manual*, which contains more detailed definition on most subjects, such as the process and products, as well as covering areas that are not included here. The *Manual* should be read before any attempt is made to introduce DSDM into an organisation.

Like all DSDM projects, the method is subject to iterative and incremental development: products are delivered and users provide feedback on what is good and what could be improved. In this case, the product is the method and the users are all those organisations that are applying the method on their projects. At the time of writing, version 2 of the method is available (DSDM, 1995). In this book, Jennifer Stapleton has extracted the essential foundations of DSDM that are not expected to change in future versions – but the users always change their minds about what they want, so time will tell.

In Part One, you will find an overview of the method, together with explanation of what is intended by the words in the *Manual*. There are several short examples of what does and does not work within projects using DSDM, together with a liberal sprinkling of Jennifer's personal views and experiences.

More lengthy case studies are contained in Part Two. These provide insight into the successes and problems that projects have encountered in the use of DSDM.

Part Three tells you how to get further information.

The book is aimed at IT staff working at all levels in the development of business applications. Because of the nature of DSDM as a controlling framework for RAD, most benefit will be gained by more senior IT staff, such as IT directors, project managers, system architects, business and systems analysts, and quality managers and auditors. However, since all DSDM team members are able to make decisions about the way a given project will operate at the day-to-day level, the readership does not exclude more junior staff. Indeed, they would probably gain considerable benefit from a wider view of what is involved in DSDM.

The text is not intended for undergraduate teaching. We feel very strongly that many of the business issues that the method addresses are unlikely to be understood by anyone who has not met the pressures and cultural constraints that IT solution providers currently face from their customers, whether internal to an organisation or external.

No preface is complete without a thank you to someone. In this case, it has to be the Consortium itself. Apart from the administrative staff at the Secretariat (who seem tireless and are extremely efficient), all the work of the Consortium is done by volunteers. Without them, the method would not exist and this book would not be possible.

Paul Taylor
Chairman
The DSDM Consortium
November 1995

Introduction

Background

For 40 years the business community has looked to the automation of clerical processes both for efficiency and to gain elusive competitive advantage. In that period, information technology practitioners have consistently failed to deliver the necessary computer applications on time and within budget or to provide the functionality needed by the business.

It has taken us 40 years to understand that business requirements change rapidly and are difficult to define and that the people who understand business processes best are the people who use them day by day. We have seen that development projects can gain a life of their own and become enmeshed in their own complexity, but we have learnt that applications development is not a black art and is amenable to structure and discipline.

During the past 10 years, there have been a number of serious attempts to understand the application development process and to codify ways in which these failures can be overcome. The UK has long been at the forefront of best practice in applications development, and it is not surprising that the most rigorous approach to modern applications development has been developed there.

In 1994, information systems professionals from large and small organisations in a wide variety of industries came together with consultants and project managers from some of the largest companies in the IT industry to form a not-for-profit Consortium. This Consortium is dedicated to understanding the best practice in application development and codifying it in a way that can be widely taught and implemented.

The result is the Dynamic Systems Development Method (DSDM), a way of developing application systems that truly serve the needs of the business. Now the method is being used on a wide variety of projects, both small and large, simple and complex, in many countries, and the Consortium continues its work to refine the content of the method.

Given that we are building business systems with some IT content, the philosophy behind DSDM is simple:

- Development is a team effort. It must combine the users' knowledge of the business requirements with the technical skills of IT professionals.
- High quality demands fitness for purpose as well as technical robustness.
- Development can be incremental. Not everything has to be delivered at once, and delivering something earlier is often more valuable than delivering everything later.
- The law of diminishing returns applies – resources must be spent developing the features of most value to the business.

DSDM is about people, not tools. It is about truly understanding the needs of the business and delivering solutions that work – and delivering them as quickly and as cheaply as possible. The method will not solve every IT problem, but it will go a long way towards ensuring that the business gets the applications systems it needs in the next 40 years.

Some definitions

The first questions to ask when coming to DSDM are 'what is it?' and 'why is it different?'. I have always found the first question quite difficult to answer. This is mostly because (despite its name) it is not a method in the accepted sense, but a framework of controls for RAD, supplemented by guidance on how to apply those controls. It is a method in as much as it defines a process and a set of products, but these have been deliberately kept at a high level so that they can be tailored for any technical and business environment. There are no prescribed techniques, but suggested paths are supplied for implementors of both structured and object-oriented approaches. It is different because it is possibly the only publicly available method that covers all aspects of system development from project inception through to support and maintenance. It addresses the needs of all participants in RAD: project managers, developers, end users, user management and quality assurance personnel.

DSDM describes project management, estimating, prototyping, timeboxing, configuration management, testing, quality assurance, roles and responsibilities (of both users and IT staff), team structures, tool environments, risk management, building for maintainability, reuse and vendor/purchaser relationships – all in the RAD environment.

Next question: what is RAD? There are many jokes about what RAD stands for – rapidly achieving disaster, really awful design – the list goes on. All of them are based on the historical view of RAD as an excuse for bypassing all the best practices in software engineering and starting to code before any real understanding of the proposed system has been reached. My view is that RAD should really stand for responsive application delivery, that is building what the business needs, when it needs it. The two parts to this definition are equally important. If the system is to meet the business needs, then it must be sufficiently robust to be usable in the operational environment. Secondly, the immediate needs of the business can probably be met in the short term and allow for delivery of additional functionality later on.

A bit of history

Businesses are putting increasing pressures on their IT suppliers to deliver better systems, faster and cheaper. In the rapidly changing world of today, they are no longer able to wait for years for a system to be provided: the business may be radically changed during the years of development. It is imperative to find a different way of building IT systems. The technology that is now available to developers allows for speedier production of systems, but the answer lies not only in the use of tools. The whole process needs to change. The classical, waterfall lifecycle does not take full advantage of modern technology and does not facilitate the change that is inherent in all systems development. The classical, waterfall lifecycle has been around for about 30 years and is basically the solution to an old problem – that of not having a full understanding of the problem to be solved and not having a coherent approach to solving the problem before starting to code a solution.

The waterfall approach of a strict sequence of stages has been seen to be flawed for some years now. Several attempts have been made to move away from it, including Boehm's (1986) iterative style of development using a spiral model of planning, risk analysis, engineering and customer evaluation. Although excellent, the spiral model did not achieve the penetration into IT practices that it deserved. Gilb (1988) has been propounding evolutionary development for many years now, but he too seems to have been a voice in the wilderness. One explanation for the majority of IT solution providers not changing their development lifecycles could be that, until very recently, there has not been sufficient pressure from their customers.

The IT industry had become increasingly aware of RAD following Martin's (1991) book, which gave some excellent pointers as to how to make RAD work but did not provide the total solution. There are many RAD tools on the market, but to use them often meant buying the vendor's process as well. This was seen as a block to the growth of RAD by the founding members of the DSDM Consortium.

The Consortium was inaugurated in January 1994 with the aim of producing a public-domain, commonly agreed method that would be tool independent. Ed Holt (now of SELECT Software Tools), who chaired the Consortium for the first two years, said that every organisation that bought a RAD tool really needed a new process. DSDM aims to provide that process for building and maintaining systems which meet tight time constraints in a controlled project environment. The Consortium had 17 founder members, who represented a mix of organisations that holds good today: large IT vendors, smaller tool vendors and user organisations of all sizes. The Consortium now has over 1000 members and is growing internationally.

During 1994, the Consortium's Technical Work Group put together the process and produced guidance material based on the experiences and best practices of Consortium members. Some components of the method were original ideas from experts in particular areas, although most of them were tried and tested but had not previously been brought together as a cohesive approach.

After version 1 of the method was published early in 1995, an early adopter programme was put in place to monitor the use of the method in practice. After feedback from the early adopters and the addition of material that had deliberately been left out of version 1 to get the method visible as soon as possible, version 2 was published in November 1995. The Technical Work Group is still collecting feedback from users of the method and addresses particular needs as they arise. through the production of white papers, which supplement the method. For instance, white papers that have been published in 1996 include DSDM in large projects and using the method as a tool during business process change.

To ensure that the method is well understood and applied correctly, the Training and Accreditation Work Group put together a training and examination process that was launched alongside version 1 and which it continues to manage. At the time of writing, over 4500 people have been trained by accredited training providers, and increasing numbers are going through the examination process to become certified DSDM practitioners.

Overview of the method

The whole method is based on nine principles, which are discussed in more detail later on, but it is useful to list them here. The first four define the foundations on which the DSDM is built and the other five provide the principles that have guided the structure of the method.

1. Active user involvement is imperative.
2. DSDM teams must be empowered to make decisions.
3. The focus is on frequent delivery of products.
4. Fitness for business purpose is the essential criterion for acceptance of deliverables.
5. Iterative and incremental development is necessary to converge on an accurate business solution.
6. All changes during development are reversible.
7. Requirements are baselined at a high level.
8. Testing is integrated throughout the lifecycle.
9. A collaborative and cooperative approach between all stakeholders is essential.

All of these principles have been found to be necessary if a quality system is to be supplied in the time-scale required by the business.

The iterative and incremental process embodied in the fifth principle consists of five phases. The first two phases are sequential: feasibility to assess the suitability of the system to the approach and to provide an initial view of the costs, etc. followed by the business study, which builds the business and technical foundations of the rest of the project. After the business study, the first of the iterative phases is the functional model iteration, in which the analysis started in the business study is done in more detail. The analysis is supported by evolutionary prototyping of functionality inside the system architecture, which is also defined at a high level in the business study. When an area of functionality is well enough understood, the design and build iteration engineers the system component to sufficient quality to be delivered in the implementation phase. Implementation covers not only moving the system to the production environment but also training the users. At the end of implementation, the increment is reviewed, and the business decision is made about what further work (if any) needs to be done in subsequent increments.

No process is complete without the people to enact it. The first principle states that the end users must be closely involved throughout development: their regular input and feedback are essential to the method. DSDM defines roles for the people involved in a DSDM project. These include both users and IT staff. For example, one user role is that of Visionary. This is usually taken by the person who is responsible for getting the project started through his or her vision for IT support in the business area. A key IT role is that of Technical Coordinator, who is basically the system architect and keeper of the technical vision. The combination of these two roles ensures that the business and technical foundations of the project are secure, but there are many more roles defined in both areas of specialism.

DSDM aims to deliver systems to time-scales that would be impossible using the waterfall approach. The impact is that the work processes have to be managed in a different way and the techniques used within those processes need to be honed down to reduce overheads as much as possible. The major instrument for controlling work is the timebox. The timebox in DSDM is a short period of time (a matter of days or a few weeks) within a project when something is produced to defined quality objectives, so satisfying the third, fourth and eighth principles. By taking a product-based view rather than an activity-based view of process, DSDM allows the controls to be focused on what is produced rather than on the method of production. This enables a flexible approach to be taken to the techniques used within the method.

Application of the sixth principle of reversible change means that everything that is produced must be controlled sufficiently well in order to move back to a known state when any product proves to be wrong.

So DSDM is about controlling a style of development, which is commonly viewed as a way of producing unmaintainable systems. It keeps a firm focus on satisfying the business needs rather than IT's perception of them. The application of DSDM's user-centred, iterative and incremental approach results in many benefits. As has been proven on many projects, these include the following:

- The users are more likely to take ownership of the system.
- The risk of building the wrong system is reduced.
- The final system is more likely to meet the users' real business require-ments.
- The users will be better trained.
- The system implementation is more likely to go smoothly.

Why is DSDM more rapid than the waterfall?

DSDM produces 'industrial-strength' systems that meet users' needs and are fully extendable and maintainable over long periods of time – they are not one-off or throw-away. In business terms, they are the exact peer of good systems developed by the waterfall approach, but take a lot less time to develop.

There are two main reasons. Less is actually done. Much less time is spent in briefing people and bringing them repeatedly up to speed. Little time is lost in task switching by users or developers. Most of all, only the features that are needed are actually developed.

The second reason is that problems, misunderstandings and false directions are identified and corrected early, so avoiding the massive rewrites often required late in waterfall projects. This has a further benefit. The resultant code developed under DSDM is consistent and of a piece, whereas waterfall code, by the end of the project, is often already patched and out of synchrony with its documentation. The result is that DSDM-delivered code is also easier to maintain.

About this book

While the *Manual* has been designed to be readable and is obviously the first port of call when the method needs to be understood in depth, it is necessarily focused on what the method contains. With the expansion of the use of the method, there has been an increasing need for something that contains practical experiences of the method in practice – rather than the theory. Hence, the DSDM Consortium has commissioned this book. It has been interesting to write: I hope you find it interesting to read.

Part One contains some explanation of the method as described in the *Manual* but, more importantly, it contains anecdotes and information from real projects.

Part Two contains some case studies, all of which have been provided by par-ticipants in the projects described. They cover what their authors felt were impor-tant aspects of their projects. They are definitely a miscellany, being of varying lengths and of varying depth of description, but I hope that you will find some-thing of value in each one.

Part Three provides information about information. It tells you about the Con-sortium, how to contact us, buy the *Manual*, find out about training and so on.

PART ONE

The method

CHAPTER ONE

DSDM process overview

1.1 Introduction

Figure 1.1 shows the development process. This is affectionately known as 'the three pizzas and a cheese'. The forward path follows the dark arrows, and recognised routes back to evolve the system are shown by the lighter arrows. As stated in the Introduction, the DSDM development lifecycle is in five phases. These are:

1. feasibility study
2. business study
3. functional model iteration
4. system design and build iteration
5. implementation.

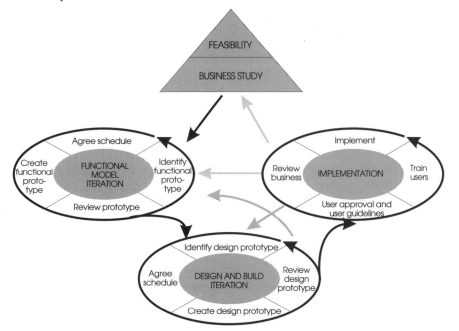

Figure 1.1 DSDM process diagram.

The feasibility and business studies are done sequentially. They set the ground rules for the rest of the development, which is iterative and incremental and, therefore, they must be completed before any further work is carried out on a given project. How the last three phases overlap and merge is left to a particular project to decide. A project team may decide to do all the functional model iterations before moving onto system design and build iterations and finally iterating through the placement of the system in the working environment. However, this approach is effectively just iterating inside the stages of a waterfall lifecycle and does not take full advantage of the flexibility that DSDM offers. Before looking at the various ways that projects have used the last three phases, we need to understand what the overall aims of the phases are and the products that are derived in each phase.

Each of the products mentioned in this chapter is considered essential to the success of a DSDM project, but the way in which they are produced and their detailed content are left to be defined in organisational standards or on a project-by-project basis. The DSDM Consortium has taken the view that to include all possible products in all possible projects could lead to slavish following of an overengineered lifecycle. This minimum set of products can be expanded but should never be reduced without good reason. Some additional products may be needed for every project in an organisation depending on local practices, but the method should be tried out on several projects before this is done to ensure that the process is not being unnecessarily overloaded.

Some method developers have taken the opposite view to that of the DSDM Consortium and tried to cater for every possibility and, as a result, have gained a name for being too lengthy in their application. Although this is a fault in the application of such methods rather than in their contents, it would be disastrous for a RAD method to become known as bureaucratic or overcomplex. DSDM hopes that, by taking a minimalist approach, careful thought will be given to the nature of each project and its inherent risks. The result should be a product set that is suited to the needs of the project under consideration.

In line with this minimalist approach, the *DSDM Manual* defines each phase of the process in terms of its purpose, preconditions, products and the roles involved. It does not supply a particular set of activities within each phase as this will depend on the application being built, the organisation building it and the organisation for whom it is being built. Similarly, products are defined in terms of their purpose and the generic quality criteria by which the products should be assessed. The actual contents will be determined by local practices, such as the preferred analysis or project management techniques.

1.2 The feasibility study

This phase is more an assessment of whether or not the DSDM approach is the right one for the project than a traditional feasibility study. This is largely because, for many feasibility studies, the waterfall approach is implicitly accepted as the default approach to development. When DSDM is offered as an alternative approach by the IT solution supplier (whether internal or external to the organisation), then care should be taken that it is indeed appropriate.

The normal considerations in a feasibility study are still present, such as a definition of the problem to be addressed together with the answers to questions such as 'Do we think the proposed system is technically possible?', 'Is the impact on the current business processes acceptable?' and the bottom line 'Is it worth doing?', but we also have to answer the question 'Is DSDM the best way to build the system?'. Some applications will be difficult to produce using DSDM, and other chapters in this book show how to decide what is and what is not amenable to DSDM. The considerations that drive this are organisational and people issues more often than not.

First and foremost, there is significant impact on the user community if the process is going to work successfully. This impact will be unacceptable to many senior managers unless there is a real business need to deliver the system within time-scales that would be considered next to impossible using other methods.

Given that DSDM is to be used for the development of systems that are urgently needed, the feasibility study is necessarily a short, sharp exercise. Some organisations are so cautious in the run-up to development that feasibility studies can take as long as two years before it is finally agreed by all parties that all the ins and outs of the problem have been considered. The DSDM feasibility study will last no more than a few weeks. Therefore, the feasibility report will cover all the usual topics, but not in great detail. If any areas are considered to be very risky, the decision has to be made as to whether or not to proceed, so there should be sufficient information to make decisions about managing that risk. The key word here is 'sufficient'. The DSDM philosophy is to do enough and no more.

As well as the feasibility report, there are two other products from the feasibility study. Both are produced to support the findings in the feasibility report. The first is an outline plan for development that will add weight to the findings that the desired outcome is achievable and the second is a fast prototype. The prototype is an optional product. Many projects will have no need to carry out this exercise. Its aim is to show that the project is technically feasible, but a key question to ask is 'Does the production of a prototype add value to the contents of the feasibility report?'. In many cases the answer will be 'no', because the business is reasonably well understood and the technology is tried and tested within the organisation. Even when either of these is not true, it is often wise not to leap into building something before the system is a little better understood. This can engender just the sort of attitude to RAD that DSDM is designed to negate, that is 'Let's build it now and not worry about the consequences six months or a year down the line'.

1.3 The business study

Having decided that DSDM is indeed the way to go, the business study provides the foundations on which all subsequent work is based, but again this is a short exercise to achieve enough understanding of the business and technical constraints to move forward with safety. As its name suggests, the prime activity here is to get a good understanding of the business processes to be automated and their information needs. To achieve this in the short time-scales of a DSDM project, this activity is very strongly collaborative. The 'usual' approach to the early stages of analysis by interviewing people separately just will not work. What is needed is a series of facilitated workshops of knowledgeable staff who can quickly pool their knowledge and gain consensus as to the priorities of the development. The result of these workshops will be the Business Area Definition that will identify not only the business processes and associated information but also the classes of users who will be affected in any way by the introduction of the system. From these user classes, the individuals who will participate in the development will be identified and agreement reached with their management as to their involvement.

The Business Area Definition is a high-level view of the processes to be automated. In a structured analysis environment, it will probably contain a data flow diagram showing the major processes but without lower level refinements of those processes (these will be produced later) and a first-pass entity–relationship diagram. In an object-oriented environment, it will probably contain a first-pass business object model. However, these are only suggestions to give a flavour of the level of detail that is expected in the Business Area Definition. They are not prescribed.

Each of the high-level functions identified in the Business Area Definition has to be prioritised so that the most important functionality will be developed in preference to less essential parts, which can be added on later if required. The prioritisation will be led principally by business need but should also take into account the technical constraints that may drive some functionality to be developed first, even though it is less important in business terms.

Because parts of the software will begin to be produced in the next phase (the functional model iteration), it is important to understand not only the functionality to be developed but also the system architecture that will be used. So another product from the business study is the System Architecture Definition, which describes the development and target platforms as well as the architecture of the software to be developed in terms of its major components and their interfaces. As with everything else produced during the business study, the System Architecture Definition is allowed to change during later work. For instance, the first-cut placement of processes in a client/server-based system could change as a result of considerations about network traffic when this is better understood. Moreover, the detail of the system design will be added and refined as work progresses.

Last but not least, the outline plan produced as part of the feasibility phase is refined to produce the Outline Prototyping Plan. This covers all prototyping activities in both the functional model iteration and the design and build iteration. It should include not only the prototyping strategy but also the configuration management plan. Configuration management assumes great importance in an iterative and incremental approach, such as that adopted by DSDM.

1.4　Functional model iteration

The focus of the functional model iteration is on refining the business aspects of the system, that is building on the high-level functional and information requirements identified during the business study. To this end, both standard analysis models and software are produced. Both the functional model iteration and the design and build iteration consist of cycles of four activities:

1. identify what you are doing in the cycle;
2. agree how you are going to go about it;
3. do it;
4. check that you did it right (by reviewing documents, demonstrating a prototype or testing part of the software).

The Functional Model, which is built up in these cycles, consists both of analysis models and of software components that contain the major functionality and will satisfy some of the non-functional requirements, in particular any related to usability. The software components and analysis models are built side by side, with the analysis models taking the lead initially. As the cycles continue, the findings of prototyping activities feed back into the analysis models and, as the models are refined, the prototypes are progressively moved towards software that could possibly be delivered but that is perhaps not as well engineered as it might be in some respects. For instance, although performance considerations should never be left until late in the development, the performance of these early software components could be less than optimal, as long as it is known how this will be addressed later.

The symbiotic development of analysis models and functioning software components is not as chaotic as it may at first appear. Later chapters will explain how it is controlled. Unfortunately, the chapters in the *Manual* for version 2 covering the process and its associated products do not stress strongly enough that the functional model contains well-constructed analysis models as well as software components. This has led to some projects doing analysis on the fly, even though later chapters of the *Manual* give quite specific guidance on the modelling activities that should take place. Careful analysis is necessary if the system is to be well founded.

It is essential that the software components of the functional model are tested as they are produced. This obviously includes unit testing, but as many other classes of testing as are possible should be undertaken. The focus of testing in the Functional Model will necessarily be on what the components do and whether or not they knit together into a usable set of functionality. Non-functional aspects are tested in the design and build iteration. This gives rise to the backwards arrow in the process diagram from the design and build iteration phase to the functional model iteration. It will often be easier, and indeed more sensible, to address the detail of an area of functionality together with its non-functional aspects in one chunk before addressing the detail of another area. The extent to which the two phases merge will largely depend on how the application breaks down into components, and the facilities of the development environment.

Other products that result from the functional model iteration at different stages of its progress are:

- **Prioritised functions**. As analysis proceeds, the detail of the high-level functions identified in the Business Area Definition is produced. Thus, the crude prioritisation that took place at that stage is progressively refined during the functional model iteration. It is this refined set of prioritised functions, which defines the core functionality, that is guaranteed to be delivered to the users at the end of the current increment.
- **Functional prototyping review documents**. As the system is iteratively reviewed by the users, the comments of reviews need to be kept. It is just as important to know what was liked and should, therefore, be retained as well as what was wrong and needs to be changed or discarded. Obviously, the review at the end of one cycle will directly lead into deciding what is to happen in the next cycle, but the review documents can be used across a wider area, even to providing useful information for later projects.
- **Non-functional requirements**. All the non-functional requirements that are elicited during the business study and the functional model iteration should be recorded. Some of these will be satisfied during the functional model iteration, but the majority of them are likely to be dealt with in the design and build iteration. These requirements will focus the activities of the design and build iteration correctly, as the development moves away from analysis to more technical issues.
- **Risk analysis of future development**. As the functional model progresses, the risks in the project will come to light more clearly, so this is a key document that should be produced. Risk analysis and management are obviously not isolated activities but run throughout every project, but by highlighting this as a point at which action should be taken DSDM is taking the view that this is about the last time that risks and countermeasures can be usefully identified and possibly dealt with, given the short time before the system or system increment must be delivered into the operational environment.

1.5   Design and build iteration

The design and build iteration is where the system is engineered to a sufficiently high standard to be safely placed in the hands of the users. The major product here is obviously the Tested System. The diagram of the DSDM process does not show testing as a distinct activity for the simple reason that testing is happening throughout both the functional model iteration and the design and build iteration. Some environments or contractual arrangements will require separate testing phases to be included at the end of the development of the increment, but this should not be the major activity encountered in the waterfall lifecycle. Testing is just as important in DSDM and has just as much effort involved in it, but it is thinly spread throughout development.

The tested system will not necessarily satisfy all the requirements identified during development, but it will satisfy all the requirements that have been agreed. The core of requirements (what DSDM calls the minimum usable subset) will, of course, be contained in the tested system, with as many other parts of the whole picture added in as time allows.

Intermediate products that come early in the design and build iteration are design prototypes and their associated design prototyping review documents. Design prototypes are intended to be evolutionary, as are the functional prototypes.

1.6   Implementation

The implementation phase covers the cutover from the development environment to the operational environment. This includes training the users and handing over the system to them. This could be as simple as placing the new system on a single PC or as complex as a major system roll-out across national boundaries. The iteration in the implementation phase is applicable when the system is being handed over to a dispersed user population over a period of time. Otherwise the phase just iterates once!

The products of this phase obviously include the delivered system that contains all the necessary documentation. The other components that make the system usable are also included: the User Manual and a trained user population. The User Manual is completed in this phase but could easily have been started earlier, and often is. Many projects have found it useful to have the user members of the team produce the user materials, while the developers are focused on more technical aspects of development. This is possible, since the users in the team understand the system, but the great advantage is that they will be able to describe how to operate it in language that the rest of the user population will understand. This can be a first for some developers.

The other product of this phase is the Project Review Document. This is produced immediately the system or system increment is deemed complete and does not replace other project review documents produced, say, six months into the operational life of the system, in which other matters are considered, such as whether or not business benefits have been achieved by the installation of the system. The Project Review Document is used to summarise what the project has achieved in terms of its short-term objectives. In particular, it reviews the requirements that have been identified during development and assesses the position of the system in relation to those requirements. There are four possible outcomes (three of which are shown by returning arrows on the DSDM process diagram in Figure 1.1). The four outcomes are:

1. All requirements have been satisfied and there is no further work currently envisaged (hence no return arrow!).
2. A major area of business functionality was discovered during development that had to be temporarily sidelined in order to deliver on the required date. This means returning to the business study and scoping another tranche of development from start to finish.
3. Lower priority functionality was squeezed out of development owing to the time-scales and will now be added in. This involves returning to the functional model iteration and working through the process from that point.
4. An area of concern in the design and build iteration was omitted, again owing to time pressure, but can now be addressed. This last point does not mean that a poorly built system was delivered, but that lower priority non-functional aspects have been omitted. For instance, a system may be delivered with a simplified access control that will suffice in the short term, but should be refined for long-term use or perhaps a non-critical area of the system has been delivered with less than optimal performance characteristics. It could have been decided that the latter was acceptable in the short term but, as volumes of traffic increase with system use, good performance will become increasingly important.

1.7 Key points

- The DSDM process provides a framework that should be populated according to organisational practices and project needs.
- The feasibility study investigates whether or not DSDM is the right approach for the project.
- The business study provides the business and technical foundations for all later development.
- The functional model iteration cycles produce both analysis documentation and working software.
- The design and build iteration engineers the system to the required level for operational use.
- After placing the system in the operational environment during the implementation phase, the scope of what has been delivered and what needs to be delivered next must be assessed.
- Testing is performed throughout the iterative phases and is not a discrete activity at the end of the development lifecycle.
- The DSDM products are defined in outline only to allow them to be used in any technical or business environment.
- The set of products is as minimal as it can be, while ensuring safe progress towards delivery and maintenance.

CHAPTER TWO

The underlying principles

The foundations of DSDM are contained in nine underlying principles. For DSDM to be successful, all of these principles must be applied in a project. If one of them is ignored, the whole basis of DSDM is endangered. Some projects may find that one or more of the principles is difficult to apply, in which case the use of DSDM should be seriously reconsidered. At the very least, an approach to mitigating the consequence of non-conformance to the principles needs to be thought out.

Each principle has an important place in the way DSDM operates. We will consider them one by one.

Principle 1   Active user involvement is imperative

Although the order of the principles has no special significance, this principle deserves its position at the head of the list because it is the most important. The user involvement in a DSDM project is not only active: it is pro-active. In many other approaches to system development, the users are involved at the beginning when requirements are elicited, then sporadically throughout the development work as products, such as functional specifications, are produced for them to review, until they come back in full swing to do the acceptance testing.

The 'normal' user resource curve resembles the cross-section of a rather uncomfortable sofa with large arms and spikes along the seat as shown in Figure 2.1.

In DSDM, the user resource curve is much flatter. If I drew a resource curve for users in a DSDM project, it would be very close to a straight line from near the start of the project to its completion, with smaller spikes when opinions are sought in workshops, demonstrations, etc. – and the curve would be much further down the scale. The process involves a few knowledgeable users who support or participate in a development team throughout the project. This is as opposed to the traditional approach of sending out documents to a mass of users for their comments and calling in a fairly large user population for acceptance testing at the end of the process. The gaps between document reviews using this approach can lead to users losing sight of the aims and progress of the development. This often leads to comments such as 'There is a spelling mistake on page 135' – rather than a critique of the content, which is what is needed.

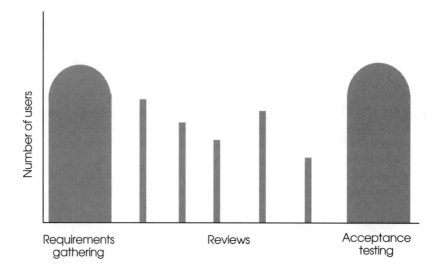

Figure 2.1 The spiky sofa curve.

Experience has shown that the total effort in a DSDM project from the user community is probably not much greater and is often the same or less. However, it is continuous and can, therefore, be more focused on the needs of the project. Moreover, because the user involvement is present over a much shorter time-frame, it can feel much greater to both the users themselves and the developers that they are working with.

Having user knowledge available at all times shortens the communication lines between the customers and suppliers of IT systems and enables work to progress much more smoothly. All too often, developers can make false assumptions about what is required on the basis of what they have understood to be true during the early stages of the project. It is this that leads to the unfortunately common scenario of users rejecting work during acceptance testing because it does not do 'what they asked for'. It is difficult for users to envisage all that they actually want. It is even harder for them to communicate their requirements to developers who, by the very nature of their work and expertise, cannot have the in-depth understanding of the business that they are trying to support.

The users should be senior enough to have an overall view of the aims of the system under development but also have detailed knowledge of what constitutes the business processes and what information is needed to support the business processes. Such users are usually important staff in their business area. This can create problems for the normal running of the business. Practical examples of how this can be handled are given in Chapter 6.

Principle 2 DSDM teams must be empowered to make decisions

In order for development to move forward quickly, the team members must be able to make quick decisions about the direction that they are taking. DSDM projects are necessarily working to tight time-scales and long decision processes that move slowly up and down the hierarchy of management will reduce the chances of delivering what is needed on time. Moreover, there is very little point in having users in the development team, if they are unable to make day-to-day decisions about what the system should do. Many DSDM projects have taken this aspect of empowerment to heart and made it work well. However, empowerment also applies to the IT members of the team.

Many managers (both business and IT) worry that they will lose control of the project, but empowerment does not mean a 'carte blanche' for staff to do as they wish. They should be given clear guidelines about where the limits lie. Of course, a major constraint on their powers is the budget for the project, and no DSDM team should be allowed to move outside that without recourse to more senior management.

Frequent small decisions can and should be made by the team. These will include:

- what the requirements mean in practice;
- whether or not the interim products of development are acceptable in terms of functionality, usability, and so on;
- the prioritisation of requirements as work progresses;
- altering the fine detail of the technical solution.

None of these will have catastrophic effects on the development. Indeed, by placing such decision-making within the team, the team members will recognise more easily what decisions must be made by other people.

It is essential not to restrict the level of empowerment so much that the team make assumptions about what to do. This can only result in the wrong assumptions being made sometimes, leading to wasted time and effort, which are at a premium in a DSDM project.

Principle 3 The focus is on frequent delivery of products

Some organisations have taken deliverables to mean operational systems, i.e. getting something out to the business in a few months as opposed to a year or so. This is not at all what the principle is about. It covers two important aspects of DSDM projects: controlling activity and working effectively in short time-scales.

By requiring frequent delivery of products, the decision-making within the team can be verified as acceptable by staff outside the team. This provides the control that some managers feel that they would otherwise lose over the direction that the project is taking. By having frequent delivery (say every week) of something tangible and visible, the safety net for reversing erroneous decisions is supplied.

Products are not just software but also other key components of development, such as a data model or a part of it. Products are just something that the team has produced as a step towards delivery of the system. More importantly, they do not need to be complete as long as they demonstrate progress and can be a basis for checking that the project is going in the right direction.

Using a product-based approach to managing projects is more flexible than a task-based one. The team members are given a fixed period of time in which to produce something that is clearly defined in terms of purpose and overall content. How they actually achieve it is left to them. For instance, they might be given two weeks to build and integrate a functional area of the system. The team members (users and developers together) then decide what activities are necessary and sufficient to deliver that piece of software to the expected quality. Compare this with the usual approach of assigning low-level tasks to individual team members. In this case, the team cannot easily change the tasks to meet the deadline. If an owner of a task hits some difficulty, the other team members are focused on their own assignments and are unable to reallocate resources to achieve the common goal.

Principle 4   Fitness for business purpose is the essential criterion for acceptance of deliverables

This principle can be reworded as 'Build the right product before you build it right'. Indeed, in version 1 of DSDM, this is what it said. However, these words were taken to mean that hacking the system together was acceptable. This is not the case. What the principle means is that the developers should not get bogged down in delivering 'gold-plated' solutions.

By focusing on fitness for business purpose, some technical issues can be left until later, if the operational characteristics are sufficiently robust in the short term. However, some technical issues will directly affect the fitness for business purpose. For instance, if an application is to be used by telesales executives taking orders, the response times must be excellent.

Traditionally, the focus of developers has been on satisfying all the requirements in a requirements document. It may well be that the requirements are inaccurate or actually unnecessary. For instance, the requirements for the telesales application may contain a blanket requirement for rapid response times. Certainly, these will be needed for the day-to-day use of the core functionality, but the need for rapid response should be questioned for the housekeeping activities in the system, if the time-scales will be endangered by trying to achieve them. These response times can be improved after the system has been installed without affecting its fitness for business purpose at the time of delivery.

Additionally, this principle focuses the quality assurance activities during development. The application of principle 3 about delivering products frequently should not drown the project in excessive checks that are not based on delivering to the business. Using fitness for business purpose as the basis for checking deliverables means that validation is probably more important than verification. In other words, looking forward to the system in use is better than checking backwards for consistency. All too often in software development, consistency with earlier products that may themselves be flawed in some way becomes the driver for acceptance of an interim product. This can lead to an inflexible approach to deciding what is going to be delivered in the end. In time-constrained projects, maximising the business benefit has to be the focus of attention at all times.

Principle 5   Iterative and incremental development is necessary to converge on an accurate business solution

With users in the team providing almost instant feedback on the work of the developers, it is possible for systems to evolve rather than take a one-pass approach to production of working software. By letting systems evolve, DSDM ensures that errors are trapped early before they become costly to correct. Moreover 'instant', if partial, solutions to business problems can be placed in the workplace, while less critical components are developed.

Even before any increment is delivered, iteration is a fact of life, as in all system development. The project manager who has never had to cope with rework of previously 'completed' products is a very lucky person indeed. When rework is not accepted as part of the development process, all signed-off work is treated as sacrosanct and protected from change. This leads to lengthy and often confrontational procedures when earlier work needs to be changed. By recognising that rework is going to happen and using an iterative process, DSDM allows developers to progress more rapidly towards the production of a system that meets the needs of the business.

The application of this principle is largely possible through the technology that is available to developers today compared with a few decades ago. This can be compared with the different technology available to military air forces. In the past, they loaded slow and cumbersome aircraft with as many bombs as possible. These would be dropped on a target that they could not guarantee to hit, particularly if the target moved. Nowadays, one more-effective missile can be launched; it can adjust its course and can be guaranteed to hit a moving target. In the waterfall approach, we fill up the requirements specification with as many things as might be needed and hope that the correct system will be achieved – even though the business needs may change during development. In DSDM, we can use the technology and the knowledge of the business to make course corrections as we go. The result is less effort for a better targeted system.

Principle 6   All changes during development are reversible

In an iterative and incremental process, it must be possible sometimes to accept that the wrong path has been taken and, therefore, to backtrack to a known safe point in development. This means that the management of all software components and their associated documents must be excellent. The *DSDM Manual* provides guidance on how this can be achieved.

Many people, on first encountering this principle, are worried that it means that large amounts of work will be discarded. This would present a serious problem if, say, the work of the past month were deemed unfit for its purpose and the project only lasted three months. However, if the other principles are applied successfully, this should not happen. In particular, the third principle of frequent delivery of products that are visible and checkable will ensure that only recent work needs to be rethought.

Principle 7   Requirements are baselined at a high level

The application of this principle within the DSDM lifecycle means that the requirements that have been captured during the business study are the agreed high-level scope of the project. By baselining (or 'freezing') requirements at this point, the detailed requirements can be elicited through the iterative process that follows. Of course further baselines can be set later in the process – and indeed they should be – to ensure that work is always working from a safe and known basis.

If requirements are not baselined before every detail has been considered, then prototyping activities will not be directed by the requirements; development can easily run out of control. An alternative outcome of not baselining early is that no software components are allowed to be produced before all the requirements have been established. This means that the users will be unable to visualise the impact of their requirements until later in the lifecycle – a return to one of the problems that DSDM is designed to alleviate.

Principle 8   Testing is integrated throughout the lifecycle

DSDM does not subscribe to the opinion of some RAD developers that testing is done at the end. This is too late and potentially disastrous. It often leads to testing being at best cursory and at worst ignored entirely owing to time constraints. Such practice is one of the contributing factors to RAD being thought of as 'quick and dirty'.

Since partial system components are produced very early on in the life of a DSDM project and evolve into the delivered system, the philosophy of DSDM is to 'test as you go'. As developers produce a software component, it is tested by themselves (for technical aspects) and the users in the team (for functional suitability). In this way, all forms of testing, including acceptance testing, are carried out incrementally throughout a project. Integration testing is performed as soon as there is something to integrate, and evolutionary development means that regression testing is very important in DSDM. Building something new that does not fit with previous components or damages the way they work should not be allowed to happen.

By demanding testing throughout development, DSDM calms the fears of IT management and business management who can be confident that the system will be fit for purpose.

Principle 9   A collaborative and cooperative approach between all stakeholders is essential

One organisation tried to remove this principle from its application of DSDM because it found it too problematical, particularly when it was contracting work to external software suppliers. The projects quickly returned to the 'us and them' attitudes that are counter to the DSDM process in which responsibilities are shared. Developers cannot divine what is needed without support from the end users.

The key words here are not only that collaboration and cooperation are important but that all stakeholders need to buy in to the approach. This means that not only must the user/developer relationships be made to work effectively, but also that different parts of the business and IT organisations must also cooperate.

Some organisations put up artificial barriers between different parts of the IT department. It is useless for the application development staff to put a system together quickly, if the operational staff do not view its take-on as important and delay it because of their own conflicting set of priorities.

IT departments are not the only culprits. A system may easily have some impact on the workings of a business area that is viewed as peripheral by the main users of the system. If their interests are not taken into account early, the whole process can founder. For instance, a large bank used DSDM to build some essential new systems without informing their financial auditors of the changes that were being made to the development process. The auditors expected certain documents to be produced during development, so that they could check the validity of the work. These documents were not present and the auditors almost came to the point of demanding that the systems be taken out of use until they were present. However, once they understood the different controls in DSDM, they were satisfied that all was well, and a major problem was averted.

This principle also has an impact when software is being built by an external supplier. Contractual arguments about what should and should not be delivered are counterproductive. Moreover, there are many organisations that have procurement departments which provide the principal contact with the suppliers. When the purchasing organisation places such barriers between the end users and the suppliers, DSDM will not work at all. Many external suppliers are using DSDM: it can work but there has to be trust on both sides – purchaser and supplier.

There must always be the ability to reach a compromise in what is to be delivered. If development is working to tight time constraints and new requirements surface, the solution providers (whether internal or external) cannot simply add them to the existing list of things to do. If they are really important, then agreement as to what can be dropped from the existing list has to be achieved. A collaborative approach is needed to ensure that what is essential will be delivered.

2.1 Key points

- The nine principles are a cohesive set and should all be applied on a DSDM project.
- The nine principles are:
    1. Active user involvement is imperative.
    2. DSDM teams must be empowered to make decisions.
    3. The focus is on frequent delivery of products.
    4. Fitness for business purpose is the essential criterion for acceptance of deliverables.
    5. Iterative and incremental development is necessary to converge on an accurate business solution.
    6. All changes during development are reversible.
    7. Requirements are baselined at a high level.
    8. Testing is integrated throughout the lifecycle.
    9. A collaborative and cooperative approach between all stakeholders is essential.

CHAPTER THREE

The process in action

3.1 When to use DSDM

DSDM is not the panacea to all project ills that developers seem perpetually to be promised. There are classes of system to which the method is most easily applied and these are the areas that an organisation, which is less experienced in RAD, should focus on to begin with – unless of course the pressure to deliver is so great that an 'unsuitable' project must be tackled before the organisation is mature in its use of RAD, and DSDM in particular. The method has been used on a wide variety of projects in a diverse set of organisations. I am loath to say that the method should never be used for a particular sort of application or platform. Whenever this sort of statement is made, someone always turns up shortly afterwards and says 'We did it!'. Indeed, BT has a motto 'You can use all of DSDM some of the time and some of DSDM all of the time'.

The method is more easily applied to business systems than to engineering or scientific applications. However, where the organisation has a good track record in building such systems, it is not impossible to apply DSDM – just a little harder because of some of the criteria involved in filtering out unsuitable systems. The *Manual* contains a suitability filter that contains questions to ask when considering the use of DSDM on a particular project. The questions are under three headings: business, systems and technical. The detail of the suitability filter is not discussed here, but the main questions to ask when deciding on the RAD ability of a proposed system are:

1. Is the functionality going to be reasonably visible at the user interface?
Of course, the user interface includes reports as well as screens or indeed any other way of showing the end user what is happening inside the system. If users are to be involved throughout the development process, they must be able to verify that the software is performing the right actions through prototyping, without having to understand the technicalities of what is happening behind the user interface.

One project that was suggested to me by a large manufacturer for their DSDM pilot did not demonstrate this characteristic. The organisation had a comprehensive system for collecting quotations from component suppliers. The system allowed buyers to enter the details of what they needed in terms of engineering specification, quantities to be provided, frequency of delivery, etc. Requests for quotes from selected suppliers were then produced by choosing 'Print'. The buyers would then stuff the paper specifications in envelopes and send them out. The organisation had decided that this process could be improved by the use of electronic messages. The only change to the process as far as a buyer was concerned would be that the final step would be a 'Send' operation, which would deliver the specifications to the suppliers electronically rather than through the mail. This operation would not be able to be verified by a buyer through inspection of the user interface. It would have been possible to capture the message for verification, but very little benefit would have been gained by this from the buyers' point of view. They only need to be assured that the messages are received at their ultimate destinations.

2.   Can you clearly identify all classes of end users? It is essential to involve users within the project who can represent all of the potential end user population. This has caused some concern when developing systems for widely disparate or geographically dispersed populations. However, with care, this is not insurmountable as will be discussed in Chapter 6. The important thing is to ensure that you can obtain complete coverage of all relevant user views within the development team. Otherwise, there is a danger of driving the development in a skewed direction. Moreover, the review process of sending out documents for a matter of weeks to a wide user group is very often not feasible on a DSDM project. Such reviews will seriously limit the chances of delivering on time.

3.   Is the application computationally complex? This is possibly one of the hardest questions to answer. What is complex for one organisation is simple for another. A lot will depend on what is available in terms of building blocks to the development team. The important thing is not to develop too much complex functionality from scratch. This question is closely linked to the first question about the visibility of functionality. For instance, if the system is performing complex actuarial calculations, this could render the project difficult for DSDM. On the other hand, if the calculation processes have been used in previous systems and are tried and tested, the actuaries will trust what is presented to them.

Just three hours after writing the previous paragraph, I attended a local DSDM Users Group meeting. I was chatting to someone who is working on a large insurance project. He said that the insurance calculation parts could not be done using DSDM. I heartily agreed with him. Immediately, someone chipped in who is working on a project for another insurance company with the comment 'The users in our team are underwriters and the developers are ex-underwriters, so we are doing everything using DSDM'. As I said at the beginning of this chapter, as soon as you say you cannot do something using DSDM, someone will be able to prove you wrong. This time it was rather quicker than usual, if you replace actuaries with underwriters!

4. Is the application potentially large? If it is, can it be split into smaller functional components? DSDM has been used and is being used to produce very large systems, but in every case it has been possible to develop the functionality in fairly discrete chunks. There are several DSDM projects in progress at the time of writing that have a development period of two to three years. This could be viewed as not being rapid application development, but increments will be delivered at regular intervals rather than waiting until everything is complete before the system is put into operation. The focus is on delivering what is most important first and what will deliver the greatest business benefit now.

If the system is large and there is no possibility of incremental delivery, i.e. everything has to be delivered in a matter of months for the system to be useful, then it must be possible to break the work down for development by parallel teams. Indeed, in large systems, there are likely to be parts that have to be developed using waterfall methods, and this will force a degree of parallel development on the project. The introduction of parallel working has significant impact on the level of control that will be needed.

5. Is the project really time constrained? It is all too easy for management to say that a system must be delivered by a certain date when they do not really mean it. This is potentially disastrous for the project. It means that, while the developers are geared up to follow the DSDM guidance, the end user participation at all levels is not as forthcoming as it should be. At best, this is frustrating. At worst, the project goes in the wrong direction because the drive from users is not there and developers start making assumptions about what is needed in order to keep active.

With users in the development team, they can see the effort that the developers are putting in. Hence, they have a greater understanding of what is possible within the time-scale. The result is that they are more willing to compromise on what will be in the delivered system. Without time constraints, they will not see any reason for compromise and will demand that everything be done. This will cause delay and inevitably the business benefits to be gained by the new system will be postponed.

6. Are the requirements flexible and only specified at a high level? This could be reworded as 'Do you have complete understanding of everything that must be delivered?'. Whatever the project, the answer is just about always 'No!' but, for DSDM to work successfully, the level of detailed understanding at the outset of the project should be lower than is the norm. This question was left out of version 1 of DSDM, and many experienced RAD developers felt that they had been cheated by the method. This has now been put right, but we need to look at why this was considered so important.

The use of prototyping with knowledgeable users to elicit requirements as you go is fundamental to the approach. If everything is understood and all the detailed requirements have been agreed and fixed before the software builders come on the scene, major benefits of DSDM will not be achieved, such as building the right system rather than what was originally requested.

Also, if the requirements are inflexible, it will not be easy to negotiate what can be left out, if the project deadline is approaching and a great deal of work remains to be done.

3.2   The reality of iteration and incremental delivery

As stated earlier, iteration is a fact of life in all IT projects. It is just that going round the same piece of work to attend to an earlier error in understanding is guarded against in traditional approaches to development. However, just because it is a fact of life, that does not mean to say that it is an easy thing to control. Many developers like the freedom that accepting iteration provides but, without the necessary controls, they can run away in the pursuit of perfection that may not actually be realisable. A non-RAD project that I encountered some years ago suffered from just this problem. It was decided that, with the move from green screens to a graphical user interface, they should use a more user-centred approach to development without thoroughly thinking through the completion criteria for their prototyping activities. The prototyping part of the project took on a life of its own and became unrelated to the other analysis and design work that was taking place in parallel. This caused enormous friction, as it became unclear as to which part of the development team had the lead at any one time.

With all prototyping activity, you must decide on the evaluation criteria that are to be used when demonstrating a prototype or putting it into the hands of the users to investigate. This has been accepted practice within the human computer interaction (true HCI!) community but has not always filtered out to the 'mainstream' developers. Fortunately, with DSDM, the timebox provides a defined scope of work, a mandated stopping point for iteration and defined completion and acceptance criteria. The use of timeboxes is discussed in more detail in Chapter 4.

DSDM has clearly addressed how to control iteration through timeboxing. It does not address the issues involved in incremental delivery. This is because incremental delivery has no distinct DSDM flavour other than the fact that not everything may be delivered in an increment. However, it may be worth a few words here about the subject.

Incremental delivery is extremely valuable in delivering quality working systems to the business faster. Nevertheless, it does increase the load on what the development team has to do. Instead of working steadily towards a single goal, there are repeated points when a complete and consistent set of documentation, working software, user manuals, training materials, etc. must be available. The effort involved in this should not be underestimated but, with the tool support available today, this is not the problem that it used to be.

3.3   Analysis and design techniques

One of the things that has contributed to the wide acceptance of DSDM is the fact that it does not mandate a particular set of techniques to be used in a RAD project.

Rather, it takes the view that RAD is about using what you know but managing the day-to-day activities of analysis, design, building and testing differently.

Hence, if we consider just analysis and design techniques for which there are a multiplicity of variations in both structured analysis and design methods and object-oriented methods, any of them can be adapted and used within the framework of DSDM. The important aspect that DSDM puts forward is to decide what constitutes the minimum set of analysis and design models necessary for the safe progression towards delivery, and the minimum set required for maintenance purposes.

The minimum set for these are defined as the core models. These will be reviewed and checked as they grow incrementally towards the final system. Many other models are used simply to sort out the ideas of the developers and therefore do not need to undergo rigorous checks to ensure that they are right. These are defined as support models. If a developer has drawn a support model in her workbook just to clarify what is happening, the time taken in reviewing it will be a bar to rapid movement towards the goal of delivery. This means that careful thought has to be given at the start of the project as to the needs of the project and maintenance.

If we consider the core models for maintenance first, the question to ask is 'What do maintenance staff need to see to carry out their job successfully?'. The first answer is a resounding cry from all maintenance staff that they trust very little beyond the code itself. So, the code must be readable and well documented so that they can see what it is supposed to do. To support the code, other useful documentation typically covers an overview of what the system does, a context diagram to show its interfaces with other systems, a description of what the components of the system are and the links between those components, the physical data structures and the design decisions that were taken and why. Anything else is likely to gather dust on the shelves. Your project may be different so this list is not prescriptive in any way. Indeed, much will depend on the characteristics of the system itself and the toolset used to develop it.

Quite often, the design decisions are viewed as unnecessary for maintenance purposes, but one project that I was involved in two years ago provides a strong argument for including them. The database designers decided not to use indexing. There was a very good reason for this, which it would be too complicated to explain without a full system description. Unfortunately, every time someone new came to look at the system, one of the first questions was along the lines of 'Wouldn't indexing be useful?'. The loop would be gone round again and again. The design decision was recorded, but it was in a short paragraph in a very large document. Maintenance staff rarely read through large documents that have become irrelevant over time; they only want to see the code. So, maintenance core models should be kept lightweight but complete enough to help new maintenance staff to understand the system as quickly as possible.

The same is true for the core models for development. Given the set of core models to be produced for maintenance, the project needs to consider what additional models need to be produced for development to move forward with a common understanding both within the team and between the team and interested external parties.

Certain models are fundamental to the process of development. For instance, in a structured analysis method working towards a new database, the data model is crucial, but many of the detailed process models can be swiftly overtaken by events. In a small system, a high-level data flow model together with a context diagram (defined above as a maintenance core model) will often be enough to support the team in understanding the external interfaces, the partitioning of processes and the sharing of data. Because analysis models and functional prototypes are being produced in parallel, as long as the code is well constructed and well documented, the detail of processes can be in the code. Again, the set of core models will depend on the characteristics of the system and the toolset used to produce it.

In an object-oriented approach, it is difficult to imagine a system without the classes defined in the core model set, but other diagrams, such as event traces, can be regarded as support models, unless there is a particularly complex or fundamental event that needs to be documented. The set selected will again depend on the application and the development tools.

The selection of core models should never be driven by the pre-existing culture. In other words, just because a particular model has always been produced by previous software development projects, it does not mean that it must always be produced in DSDM projects. What must be decided is which documents are essential. The set of core models can be very small in DSDM because many of the documents that are produced before the introduction of the method are there to pass ideas from one class of team to another. Analysts produce detailed analysis models to pass their ideas on to the users for agreement and to designers as the basis for their work. Designers produce design documents to ensure that programmers do exactly what is necessary. Programmers produce detailed program specifications so that the designers can agree that they are doing the right thing and so that testers know what needs to tested. And so on. And so on.

A DSDM team is a fixed team containing users and developers who have between them all the major analysis, design, programming and testing skills required. As a result, the need for documents to pass ideas around is lessened. An additional benefit is that the common complaint from analysts that their work has been ignored and the counter complaint from programmers that the analysis work was a waste of time and had to be discarded are both non-existent in a DSDM project. The important different views from different roles are available throughout development.

3.4	**Key points**

■ DSDM is particularly suited to business applications that demonstrate the following characteristics:

continued over

Key points continued

1. are interactive, with the functionality visible at the user interface;
2. have a clearly defined user group;
3. are not computationally complex;
4. if large, possess the capability of being split into smaller functional components;
5. are time constrained;
6. have requirements that are not too detailed or fixed.

- Iteration is controlled within DSDM through timeboxing and does not run away in an uncontrolled manner.

- Incremental delivery can deliver business benefit early but it introduces additional work on deliverables.

- DSDM does not mandate any set of development techniques.

- Core models provide the minimum set of documentation necessary for safe progress through development and for ease of maintenance.

- The core models and support models for development and maintenance need to be agreed before development begins.

- Core models need to be reviewed for content and accuracy; support models do not.

CHAPTER FOUR

Time versus functionality

4.1 Fitting quarts into pint pots

Keeping within time-limits does not mean working faster or for longer hours than would normally be the case. Yes, the pressures will be there to work very hard and, indeed, as the project progresses, the chances are that developers will occasionally work very long hours to meet their deadlines, but this can happen on any project, whatever the method being used. Long working hours should not be taken as the norm for DSDM developers. The aim should be to work within the normal working day and to keep weekends and evenings free. To do this, you need to change the way that work is managed at all levels: the project, the team and the individual.

At the project level, the focus is on ensuring that the scope does not expand beyond what is achievable. It is essential to get the scope clearly agreed during the business study. This is the basis for all decisions about what is possible in the time available. It often happens that during the later phases, as the users get a better understanding of what the system will do for them, they ask for more things to be added in. When this happens, it is not the project manager's job to reach for the change control procedures and to enter into negotiations for more staff or more time. The time has been fixed for whatever reason, and bringing in more staff will endanger the delivery on the agreed date. Brooks (1975) stated this and it is still thought to be a solution! He pointed out that, if you bring new staff on to a project, time will be spent bringing them up to speed with the rest of the team. This must be done at the cost of the work that the original team members were planned to do.

So we do not ask for more staff and we do not ask for more time. The only thing that can happen is that, if the new request is really necessary, something gets left out of the work that was originally envisaged. We certainly do not want to let quality suffer, so the work that is left out is delivering some of the originally agreed functionality. Section 4.3 shows how to do this using the MoSCoW rules.

At the team level, the priorities of the functional and non-functional requirements are used to decide what the team should be doing at any one time. As an empowered group of people, they can decide on what work needs to be done and by whom. The team members work together to satisfy the highest priority requirements. Having regular and frequent team meetings is essential to ensure that the development is on track. Daily meetings of half an hour may initially be seen as an unnecessary overhead on the 'useful' work, but I have found that many issues can be resolved very quickly in them, and they make the staff think of themselves as a team rather than a set of individuals. The daily meetings are really a formalisation of the chat by the coffee machine, where it is well known that good ideas and expert knowledge can be gathered from other people. If the team opts for weekly meetings, a week's work from one person may be found to be in conflict with something that somebody else is doing and will have to be revisited. It is no good thinking that people will automatically talk to each other just because they are in the same team.

The worst example of uncommunicative (and therefore uncollaborative) teams that I have come across was a non-RAD project in which a team of four analysts was working at a group of four desks with no partitions between them. So, they were facing each other all day, but they did not talk! Three of them were doing the process analysis and one was assigned to data analysis. When I met them, they had been working for three months and the project was experiencing considerable slippage. None of the process analysts had discussed the interfaces of their process areas with the others, and the data analyst was working completely separately from the rest of the team. Not surprisingly, they had all gone over much the same ground and had wasted considerable effort in resolving issues that were common to them all. Even weekly meetings would have helped this unfortunate group who were carrying out personal tasks set by the project manager rather than working as a team.

At the individual level, the developers and the users have to accept that it is not possible to do everything. Developers, who want to investigate every single detail of an issue and focus on the automated system because that is what they understand and who cannot move to only doing what is absolutely necessary to the business, will find DSDM a very stressful way of working. Not only that, they will also disrupt the activities of other team members who are more user focused and who accept that doing enough is the winning strategy. Unfortunately, there is no way of knowing whether a developer will take to DSDM until it has been tried. Some people take to the ideas immediately. Others take a month or so. One DSDM project I worked with was severely handicapped by keeping on a developer who had an excellent track record in programming and was very quick to learn new technical skills, but who just could not handle the fact that he had occasionally to limit his view of what was necessary. Worse still, he viewed the users changing their minds about something as a major irritation that stopped him doing what he was there to do – design, build and test programs. The attributes of RAD developers are discussed in Chapter 8.

4.2 Timeboxes

There are several current definitions of timeboxes. One that is prevalent is the time between the start and end date of the project. The end date is inviolable and a system will be delivered on that date. DSDM has taken the concept of timeboxes further by nesting them within the project's overall timebox to provide a series of fixed deadlines by which something will be delivered, where the 'something' could be an analysis model (partial or otherwise), a part of the front end, a completed area of functionality, a combination of these or indeed anything that moves the project nearer its target of delivering a useful system on a given date.

In DSDM, timeboxes are typically between two and six weeks in length: the shorter the better. However, the limits are not inviolable. One over-zealous project auditor raised an objection to a timebox that was planned to be seven weeks long. This did not matter as long as the project manager and his team agreed that that was the minimum time required to do the work. The major advantage of keeping timeboxes short is that it is easier to imagine what can be done in the time.

It takes nine months to have a baby. While they are waiting for the baby to be born, parents will spend a considerable amount of time choosing clothing, a cot, a mobile to hang over the cot, cuddly toys, etc. If, however, parents were told that they could expect a baby in one week, they would focus attention on what they could purchase during the week and be sure of having the essentials ready for the new arrival. It is this style of thinking that makes timeboxing an effective way of carrying out successful projects in short time-scales. For some reason, it is far easier to envisage what you can do in a short period of time than to be given a task and then decide how long it will take you to do it. Hence, the timebox is a useful tool in the process of estimating the resources needed to achieve the operational system.

An important aspect of timeboxes is that they are not activity based. The aim of a timebox is to make something. How that thing is put together will be decided by the people doing the work. This is one way that the third DSDM principle about focusing on frequent delivery of products is applied.

4.3 MoSCoW rules

You will not find the MoSCoW rules in the *DSDM Manual*, but they have been adopted by many organisations using DSDM as an excellent way of managing the relative priorities of requirements in a RAD project. They are the brainchild of Dai Clegg of Oracle UK, who was one of the early participants in the DSDM Consortium.

MoSCoW is an acronym for the prioritisation that the requirements are assigned. The 'o's in MoSCoW are just there for fun. The rest of the word stands for:

■ **'Must have'** for requirements that are fundamental to the system. Without them the system will be unworkable and useless. The 'must haves' define what DSDM calls the minimum usable subset.

■ **'Should have'** for important requirements that would probably be classed as mandatory in less time-constrained development, but the system will be useful and usable without them.

■ **'Could have'** for requirements that can more easily be left out of the increment under development.

■ **'Want to have but will not have this time round'** for those valuable requirements that can wait till later development takes place.

All of these requirements are needed for the full system. The 'wish list' does not appear in the categorisation. The important thing about the MoSCoW rules is that they provide the whole basis on which decisions are made about what the developers will do over the whole project and during any timebox within the project.

To give a practical example of applying the MoSCoW rules, we could consider building a domestic video cassette recorder. The 'must haves' (i.e. the minimum usable subset) would be recording television programmes, rewinding tapes and playing them. The VCR just will not operate without these capabilities. The 'should have' would be the facility to record while away from the home. This definitely enhances the value to the user, but the VCR will be usable without it. The 'could haves' would be facilities such as fast forwarding and pausing. They add to the ease of use but are not essential. The 'want to haves' would be a remote control, automatic tracking, etc. All of which could be added later.

4.4 Controlling timebox activity

Given the above, timeboxes are really requirements satisfaction boxes in which something will be achieved. Each timebox will typically pass through three phases. These are given in the *Manual* as applying specifically to prototyping activities, but the three phases can be applied with equal success in the production of any project deliverable (Figure 4.1). The three phases are:

■ **Investigation** in which a quick first pass is made to check that the activities inside the timebox are going in the right direction.

■ **Refinement** in which the results of the investigation are improved and as much of the deliverable is produced as is possible in the time.

■ **Consolidation,** which is the final part of the timebox. Here, the aim is to make the deliverable complete and consistent within itself and, if it is part of the timebox's objectives, to check that it fits with other deliverables.

Each of these three phases starts with an objectives setting meeting with all members of the team who are participating in the timebox and finishes with a

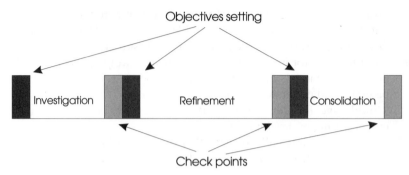

Figure 4.1　Timebox schematic.

check as to how those objectives are being met. Depending on the deliverable, this check could be a review, a demonstration or formal testing. If at all possible, the end dates for each phase should be fixed in the same way that the end of the timebox is fixed.

The parts of the phase, as shown in the development process framework diagram for the functional model iteration and the design and build iteration, are identify what you are going to do, agree how to do it, do it and check that you did it (and obviously you should be able to show that you checked that you did it).

The objectives setting meeting for the start of the timebox is the most critical. It is at this point that the team considers what the timebox was originally planned to produce. People attending this meeting will be the timebox team (developers and users) and any other necessary party, such as the Technical Coordinator and, if the timebox is particularly critical to the success of the project, key individuals, such as the Visionary.

The first task of this meeting is to review what has been achieved in any previous timebox that delivered related products and to check for any impact on the work of the current timebox. Some of the dependencies may cause the deliverables from the current timebox to be rethought. For instance, it may be that previous work has identified the need for a new mandatory component or, conversely, that a part of the planned deliverable in the current timebox does not have the necessary prerequisites to allow it to be delivered.

Having checked the deliverables for the timebox, the relative priorities of the parts of the timebox deliverable are reassessed to see whether or not they are still valid, and their relative priorities are checked and possibly reassigned using the MoSCoW rules.

Another key decision made in this initial objectives setting meeting is what the various quality criteria are that the deliverable must demonstrate to be acceptable at the end of the timebox. In the case of a timebox delivering a software component, this would be defining the test cases that will be applied but not writing the detail of tests. This cannot be done at this time, since it is not known exactly what functionality the software component will finally contain – particularly true of the 'should haves' and 'could haves'. A new 'must have' could arise during the timebox and displace some 'must have' that is seen to have a lower priority in reality.

Having done all this, the initial meeting has to agree that at least the minimum can be delivered. If not, then a quick decision has to be made about what should be done. This could involve replanning and reprioritisation of remaining work.

It is very important that not all things to be done in the timebox are 'must haves'. If they are, the content of the timebox should be revisited. The team must feel confident that, if things do not go entirely to plan, there is something that can be left out while they focus on sorting out the essential components of the timebox deliverable.

The last part of this important objectives setting session is to agree what the investigation phase will deliver.

At the end of the investigation phase, the checkpoint assesses the initial deliverable and notes any necessary changes to the timebox deliverable or its acceptance criteria that may arise. Back to back with this checkpoint, the objectives are set for the refinement phase. It is in this phase that the real meat of the timebox deliverable is tackled. At its end date, the checkpoint again assesses progress.

The final phase of consolidation starts with an objectives setting meeting that decides what must be done in the remaining time to ensure that the deliverable will be useful. The checkpoint at the end of consolidation is the final checkpoint of the timebox, and it is here that the overall quality criteria set at the beginning of the timebox will be demonstrated to have been satisfied.

How timeboxes are controlled from the project management point of view varies from organisation to organisation. Two examples of timebox control documentation that have been used are included here. One was used by the Department of Health in its pilot DSDM project. This project had done some extensive analysis before the decision to move to DSDM was made, so this form very much concentrates on controlling the design and build aspects of the system that produced statistics about the usage of certain parts of the services of local health authorities. The second one was used by Logica in a very successful project for Shell Exploration and Production. It bundles one or more timeboxes into a workpackage to be assigned to a group of people within the team. Logica also documented very clearly how timeboxes should be run and managed. Their document is contained in Appendix A.

Neither of these forms is considered to be the definitive answer to all timebox controls. Interestingly, the project manager with the Department of Health works for FI GROUP, which is arguably the largest third-party software maintenance supplier in the UK, and she included the maintainability target. So the message is 'Control what is important to you'.

Timebox specification (Department of Health)

Function to be prototyped:	Reference in functional specification:
Start date: End date:	Technical effort allowed:
Dependencies:	
Objectives (1) (2) ….	
Outcome:	
Priorities (1) (2) ….	
Outcome:	
Criteria (1) (2) ….	
Outcome:	
Agreed minimum usable subset (cross-reference to objectives):	
Performance target (1) (2) ….	
Outcome:	
Maintainability target	
Outcome:	
Quality review method	User sign-off after 3rd iteration; Technical review of code by:
1st iteration (date): 2nd iteration (date): 3rd iteration (date):	………………… (Record initials of those present)
Documentation updated: RQ (date) FS (date)	
Deliverable produced:	(File name/version no.)
Filed in:	(Library)

Timebox specification (Logica/Shell Exploration and Production)

Super-WP-manager

The normal project standards will apply to all work except as follows:

Tick if continued ☐

Signed by super-WP-manager to denote delegation of responsibility: _____ Date:

Signed by WP-manager to denote acceptance of responsibility: _____ Date:

Item no.	Item description (component of WP)	Date required	Date complete	Signed (user)	Signed (WP-manager)
	Summary – timebox 1				
	WP start date : 01 Jan 1996				
	Total effort: NN days				
	Developer 1: ABC Effort:				
	Developer 2: XYZ Effort:				
	Other tasks: MM days				
	WP end date: 04 Jan 1996				
	Review milestones				
	Agree objectives and scope	01 Jan 1996	01 Jan 1996	XYZ	ABC
	Review initial prototype	02 Jan 1996	02 Jan 1996	XYZ	ABC
	Review second prototype	03 Jan 1996	03 Jan 1996	XYZ	ABC
	Final review	04 Jan 1996	04 Jan 1996	XYZ	ABC
	Summary – timebox 2 or 1B				
	WP start date: 05 Jan 1996				
	Total effort: NN days				
	Developer 1: ABC Effort:				
	Developer 2: XYZ Effort:				
	Other tasks: MM days				
	WP end date: 08 Jan 1996				
	Review milestones				
	Agree objectives and scope	05 Jan 1996	05 Jan 1996	XYZ	ABC
	Review initial prototype	06 Jan 1996	06 Jan 1996	XYZ	ABC
	Review second prototype	07 Jan 1996	07 Jan 1996	XYZ	ABC
	Final review	08 Jan 1996	08 Jan 1996	XYZ	ABC
	Tick if continued ☐				

Signed by super-WP-manager   **Signed by project managers**

                                  Shell: Date:

Date: Logica: Date:

The tabular part of the Logica form is just the tip of the iceberg. It continues with a textual description of the status of the workpackage, which should be updated on a daily basis with progress, results, issues, etc. For completeness, the skeleton for this document follows.

1.   Users and schedule

1.1   Users

User	Responsibility
ABC	Super-WP-Manager
XYZ	User review

1.2   Changes to users
       (Changes to users and/or responsibilities)
1.3   Schedule
       (Shows key dates and who is responsible. Should show deliverables from users if these are key to the completion of the timebox – sample milestones are shown)

Step	Who	Date	Effort
Timebox 1			
Agree the initial scope, objectives and schedule	XYZ, ABC, PQR	01 Jan	
Review prototype X	XYZ, ABC, PQR	02 Jan	
Review prototype Y	XYZ, ABC, PQR	03 Jan	
Design review	TEAM	04 Jan	
Closeout review		05 Jan	

Step	Who	Date	Effort
Timebox 2, etc.			
Agree the initial scope, objectives and schedule		06 Jan	
Review storage prototype		07 Jan	
Review retrieval prototype		08 Jan	
Design review		09 Jan	
Closeout review		10 Jan	

2.   Objectives

2.1   Original objectives
       (List of BUSINESS objectives and priority: must have; should have; nice-to-have)
2.2   Changes to objectives
       (Changes to business objectives and dates)

3.   Scope
3.1   Original scope
       [Prioritised (must have; should have; nice-to-have) list of requirements
       (taken from project list of requirements)]
       (Textual description)
       (Things excluded from scope)
3.2   Refinements to scope
       (Updates to prioritised list of requirements)
       (Textual description)
3.3   Changes to scope
       (Functions to be added/removed from the prioritised list of require-
       ments)
       (Textual description)

4.   Issues
4.1   Issues index and status
       4xxx.01 An issue that is open (OPEN)
       4xxx.02 A second issue that has been resolved (RESOLVED)
4.2   List of issues

       4xxx.01   Title of issue 1 (OPEN)
       (Brief description of issue. Refer to Appendix B for any extended
       discussions)
       (Actions)
       (How resolved)

       4xxx.02   Title of second issue (RESOLVED)
       (Observations raised for new functions outside this timebox)

5.   Reviews and testing
5.1   Reviews

Review	Who	Role	Date
Review initial prototype	X		9 Feb
	Y		
	Z		
Review analysis			12 Feb
Review …			13 Feb
Review design			19 Feb
Closeout review			20 Feb

(Summary of results of the review. Reference issues raised, changes and refinements to
scope, etc.)

5.2   Tests
5.2.1 Tests at review point n

(Test 1 summary)
(Baseline ref.)
(Reference to test material)

(Test 2 summary)
(Baseline reference)
(Reference to test material)

5.2.2 Tests at review point n
(etc.)

6.   Close-out summary
(Developer's comments)
(Minimum functionality reached: yes/no?)
(Functions not completed and functions/issues outstanding. Functional,
 design, maintenance)
(User comments)
(Project managers' comments)
(Resolution of outstanding functions/issues. Defer, return to project
 prioritised list of requirements. Follow on timebox necessary?)

Appendix A   Analysis and design

Appendix B   Discussion of issues

Appendix C   Test summaries

4.5 To timebox or not?

Some activities that are essential to the success of a project are just not possible
using the timebox approach. It is not acceptable, for instance, to have only part of
the interface between the client and the server working. One of DSDM's early
adopters' projects was the development by Sysdeco of a newspaper production
tracking system by Sysdeco (UK) for the *Boston Globe*. The system was developed
from scratch in four months using DSDM, after an attempt by another organisation to tailor an existing system had failed after 18 months. DSDM was used for
the user-facing components of the system, but it was also necessary to build a data
daemon that would transfer status information from existing systems through standard interfaces. The data daemon that would perform this function had to be 100%
complete or it would be useless. Moreover, there was no simple way of involving
users in the validation of its functionality. Therefore, it was developed in parallel
using more traditional development methods. DSDM should not be used to the
exclusion of all other methods and definitely not where it is inappropriate.

4.6 The disaster scenario

The crunch question that is always asked about timeboxes is 'What happens when a major new 'must have' surfaces during development and there is no slack left in the other requirements?'. The questioner almost always seems to expect the answer that time will have to slip to accommodate the new requirements. Fortunately, this is not the answer. What happens in practice is that a swift renegotiation of the priorities is undertaken with all interested and influential parties involved. I have to say that in all the projects (bar one) that I have come across, the new 'must have' has never turned out to be a showstopper as far as the time-scales are concerned. If the system really does need it, then something will be done to fit it in. This usually means that something else has to go. In the only project I have seen in which time-scales did have to slip, the management decided that the time slippage was more acceptable than delivery of a system without what they had asked for. This was possible because the business need for the earlier date had disappeared. Wherever time is of the essence, something is left for delivery a few weeks later. The first increment will perform the short-term solution for later modification.

British Airways have been doing RAD for several years now and they have had only one RAD project fail to deliver on time. That failure was nothing to do with requirements but was to do with a key user who was difficult to get hold of when important decisions had to be made.

4.7 Key points

- Short timeboxes within the overall project timebox are the means of controlling the quality of interim products and avoiding scope creep during development.
- Keeping timeboxes short facilitates effort estimation.
- Timeboxes have a cycle of investigation, refinement and consolidation.
- All requirements are prioritised to ensure that the most essential requirements are satisfied first.
- The deliverables from a timebox are tested and/or reviewed within the timebox, rather than afterwards.
- Activity within timeboxes should be defined in terms of deliverables rather than tasks.
- Some development activities cannot be managed using the timebox approach.

CHAPTER FIVE

The RAD project manager in action

What is different?

Since time is fixed and resources are mostly fixed, the project manager's job is somewhat different from that in a traditional project with a more relaxed time-scale. All the skills that make a good project manager are still required, but the focus is slightly different. Moreover, with an empowered team, the more autocratic project manager has no place heading up a DSDM project. The responsibilities of the project manager are the same: careful planning, close monitoring of progress, keeping the team working effectively, awareness of the risks to be managed, etc. What is different is the way that planning is carried out, how progress is monitored, the style of management for an empowered team and what the specific risks are in a RAD project.

The DSDM project manager has a significant logistical challenge. There are a multitude of shorter tasks involving more parties than usual over a very confined time-frame. It is the responsibility of the project manager to ensure that all the right facilities are in place at the right time for the team to work effectively. For instance, the time between the start of analysis and the building and testing of software is very short – the facilities for these different activities must be in place when they are needed. There is very little room for logistical delays in a RAD project.

One area in which project managers traditionally spend a lot of effort is on trying to prevent drift from specifications that have been signed off. This leads to strongly enforced change control procedures. DSDM is all about enabling change to occur without the confrontation that has often arisen through adherence to a specification. Project managers who are new to DSDM worry a great deal about how to stop the scope expanding beyond what is achievable in the overall timescale of the project. I hope that the previous chapter on timeboxing has laid many of the concerns about controlling the scope to rest. I can only assure the novice DSDMer that it does work and has been proven on many projects.

| 5.2 | **Planning a DSDM project** |

DSDM defines two points in the process where project planning activities are undertaken.

1. As part of the check on the feasibility of the project, an outline plan is produced to provide confidence that the project has the likelihood of success.
2. During the business study, more information is available about what has to be done and what the relative priorities of the work components are.

Before leaving the business study, the outline plan produced during the feasibility phase is refined to take account of the additional information. Since the next stages will be the development of the system through prototyping activities within timeboxes, this refinement is called the Outline Prototyping Plan. It is outline because, until work is actually under way, it will be very difficult to say what the detailed activities will be within a given timebox. Also, the dependencies between timeboxes may make it impossible to carry out some planned work because the preceding requirements have been left out of a timebox.

The functionality to be delivered will have been identified by the end of the business study. Clear prioritisation must be achieved during the business study.

All functionality should be placed into functional groupings, which should be kept as small as possible. Each grouping should have its components clearly prioritised so that it is possible to leave lower priority parts out of the grouping, if all does not go to plan. None of this prioritisation can be done by either the project manager or the project manager with the developers on their own, as the business imperatives are what drives this decision-making process. Indeed, leaving it to the IT staff can lead to a technology-driven approach, which will not facilitate working with the users to deliver the system.

However, design considerations may occasionally over-ride business considerations as to what is most important. Some functionality will necessarily appear in more than one functional grouping. For instance, a simple enquiry as to the status of a particular item may appear in several business processes. Functionality that appears regularly in several areas is probably fundamental to the success of the system and assumes a high priority, however trivial it may seem to the overall business processes.

Other functions that are obviously given a high priority are those that are seen as critical to the success of the increment. However, this criticality should never be taken at face value. The question to ask is 'Is there a possible workaround if this functionality is not available?'. If the answer is 'yes', the functionality is assigned as low a priority as possible.

The aim of prioritisation is to ensure that the 'must haves' are as small a set as possible with the other levels of optionality well understood.

The prioritised functionality also provides the basis for deciding what architectural components must be present in the delivered system. For instance, if it is essential that some information from another system is available, then the interface to that system must be possible.

The architectural components should ideally be available before the functionality that needs them are built. Therefore, the prioritisation of the functionality will drive the prioritisation of the system architecture components. However, there will be some components that are acknowledged as important but that cannot be aligned to particular system operations. Some non-functional requirements (such as performance) may well have architectural impact that cannot be assigned to one area of functionality. When these are to be addressed and their relative priorities will depend on when they can easily be fitted in with other work.

The architectural requirements should be as clearly prioritised as the functionality. There should always be the possibility of moving away from a previously agreed technical approach, if things prove difficult. For instance, in a modelling project for an oil company, the developers were having real problems with getting the modelling tool that they were using to provide the right statistics. It was, in fact, buggy. So, given that the timebox was nearing its end date, the developers swiftly moved to providing the information through a spreadsheet for manipulation by the users: a less sophisticated solution but one that was acceptable in the short term. It was also acceptable within the architecture, since the chosen spreadsheet was part of the standard platform for the end users.

Some non-functional requirements may apply across all work, such as usability or maintainability. It is useful to assign these requirements to every timebox, since they will keep the developers focused on the overall quality objectives of the project.

There are several schools of thought about what to do first. One is that tackling something easy first gives the developers a boost and encourages further work. The problem with this approach is that it leaves the difficult areas until later and providing solutions to these may invalidate some of the earlier work.

Another approach is to identify the major technical risks in the increment and to tackle these first. This has the advantage that, if something needs to be re-thought, then there is time to do it. However it can mean that key business issues are not addressed early enough.

A third approach is to produce something that is fundamental to the business requirements. This will provide the users with early visibility of the developing system and will enable them to verify that the right direction is being taken. For systems with little technical risk, this is the best approach.

Where the technical risks are high, a combination of the second two approaches should be used, spreading the technical risks across the first few timeboxes, while delivering as much visible functionality as possible within that constraint.

As with any project plan, the project manager should identify what human resources are to be used. The users should be assigned to the areas of functionality that fit their business knowledge. Given their advisory role, they can be assigned to more than one concurrent timebox. Developers should never be assigned to more than one timebox at a time. Furthermore, if developers are from a general resource pool and have other calls on their time, the successful delivery of the products of a timebox is unlikely. The project manager should strive for dedicated technical staff wherever possible. The tight time-scales of a timebox make external activities a significant risk to completion.

Having decided on the order in which parts will be delivered and who has the relevant skills (technical and business), the next task is to allocate the work to a set of timeboxes. A crude first pass is achieved by simply dividing up the time after the business study into timeslots of, say, two weeks. Each timeslot is potentially N timeboxes, where N is the number of parallel timeboxes that are possible with the resources available.

Each timeslot should have allocated to it a mix of mandatory and less essential work that makes a sensible group of related products. How each group is chosen is totally dependent on the application under development and the architectural and business dependencies that have been identified earlier. Nevertheless, a mixture of 'must haves', 'should haves' and 'could haves' is essential to the timebox approach. If everything to be produced in a timebox is a 'must have', there is no room for manoeuvre, if things do not go well in the timebox.

Of course, all the usual project planning constraints need to be considered, such as holidays and the availability of hardware and software. If it is possible that users will be unavailable for participation in a particular timebox, there must be a decision escalation route in place. How this will work will depend on the culture and organisation of the business.

Having allocated work to the initial timeslots, the next step is to test the feasibility of the plan with the developers who will carry out the work. The question to ask here is whether or not an arbitrarily chosen number of days is sufficient for the work to be achieved.

The key is not to allow them to lengthen the timeslots by building in contingency. The contingency is already contained in the fact that not everything is necessarily delivered. If the developers want a timeslot lengthened, they should be able to justify the extra time. It is common for the first timeslot to be longer because of necessary groundwork to get the work under way. However, this should not be necessary if a known environment is being used, a 'standard' system architecture is being applied and the business functionality is not too complex.

Where the duration is accepted as sufficient, the developers should be asked if they can reduce it and still be reasonably sure of delivering the work.

If the project manager is as technically expert as the development team, it may be possible to refine the durations without reference to the developers. However, this can lead to the developers feeling that unrealistic time-scales have been imposed on them.

It is possible that the plan now extends beyond the end date for the project. In which case, the resourcing levels need to be rethought, the scope of the project needs to be revisited or the relative priorities of deliverables needs to be reconsidered. The business needs will be paramount in this process.

The detail of when the deliverables from timeboxes will be reviewed, tested and accepted is left until the timebox is initiated. However, overall procedures for these activities need to be in place. If these are either not standard to the organisation or not already agreed for the project, they should be documented now and associated through document management procedures to the timebox plan.

In addition to who will carry out the day-to-day work within a timebox, the people who will be responsible for monitoring and control of the activity must be nominated, as must the people who will have the authority to accept work from the timeboxes.

A normal project planning tool can be used to show some components of the plan: resources, parallel working in timeboxes and time-scales. This should be supported by documentation to show the optionality of work within the timebox. This can be a simple table showing, for each timebox, 'must haves', 'should haves' and 'could haves', or timebox control sheets, such as those shown in the previous chapter, can be produced in skeleton form now.

5.3 The project roles

A DSDM team consists of developers and users working together. DSDM defines several roles within a DSDM project, some of which are for IT staff and some for the users. A team is kept small in order to shorten the communication lines between team members. Typically, a DSDM team consists of two to six people. The minimum is two because there must be one person from IT to do the technical work and one user to ensure that the work will satisfy the business needs. The maximum is six because this is what has been found to be the limit beyond which the RAD process has difficulties. A project may, of course, have more than one team.

No distinction is made between the different IT roles: analysts, designers, programmers, testers, etc. They are all categorised as senior developers and developers. Senior developers are not necessarily those traditionally seen as senior, e.g. analysts, but they are developers who will lead the work in some way. A senior developer could be the best programmer on the team. The distinction is made only on experience of the type of work to be undertaken and, specifically, on experience of working in a RAD environment.

A key IT role is that of Technical Coordinator. This role defines the system architecture, is responsible for ensuring that the project is technically consistent and that all work produced is of sufficient technical quality. The role is also responsible for ensuring that technical controls, such as configuration management, are used effectively.

Being a user-centred approach to development, DSDM has defined several user roles to work both as part-time advisers and to participate within the project team. The key user role within the team is the Ambassador User. Ambassador Users are so named because they operate in very much the same way as diplomatic ambassadors. They have the responsibility of bringing the knowledge of the user community into the team and disseminating information from the team to the rest of the users. They are not the sort of full-time staff used in some organisations as an information channel between the developers and the users. An Ambassador User comes from the community that will use the delivered system.

DSDM defines another key user role, that of the Visionary. The Visionary is probably the person who initiated the project through their vision for IT support in their business area. The Visionary may not be the purse-holder and ultimate decision-maker in the business area – that is the role of Executive Sponsor. The Visionary participates early on in the project (during the feasibility and business study) to ensure that the right decisions are made as to what is important and what is not. Later, the Visionary participates in key demonstrations and meetings to ensure that the team does not lose sight of the original business objectives.

Users have traditionally sat outside the development team, providing their knowledge during requirements gathering, reviewing work in progress and performing acceptance testing. The number of users who can be involved in these activities can be quite large in order to cover all necessary user views. DSDM recognises that the holders of the Ambassador User role may not cover all necessary viewpoints, so an additional role of Adviser User is defined to cover the disparate views that may exist. Adviser Users are anyone who has an interest in the final system. This could include IT staff, such as system administrators, or 'fringe' business staff, such as financial auditors. Adviser Users will be involved on an *ad hoc* basis as required by the needs of the project.

The detail of all these roles together with their responsibilities and required skills are contained in the *DSDM Manual*. A skill common to all roles is that of effective communication. Developers of all types must be able to listen effectively and communicate their ideas in non-technical language. Users must be competent in expressing their own needs and the vision of the business.

5.4 Project structures

A typical DSDM project will have one or two teams, but a large project can grow to as many as six teams, all working in parallel. Again, like the maximum team size, six seems to be the limit beyond which things start to get unmanageable.

Where there is only one team, the Technical Coordinator role will be within the team and is likely to be carried out by the most senior technical expert. Where there are two or three teams, the Technical Coordinator role may still be filled by just one person, but that person will be outside the teams, working in a managerial and technical advisory capacity. When the project has more teams, the role of Technical Coordinator will probably be split between different IT staff. One possible way of splitting the role on a large project would be to have three people taking up different parts of the role: one would be the system architect, one would be responsible for assuring the technical quality of what is produced and the other for controlling the developing software and document configuration.

With multiple teams, it is often useful to have one team doing coordination work. For instance, one team could take the role of database administrator. Some DSDM projects have opted to have a separate testing team. This is difficult to make work successfully in 'vanilla DSDM', since every software deliverable from a timebox should have been tested within the timebox to demonstrate whatever objectives had been set for the timebox. The objectives could demand elements of system testing, integration testing and regression testing – not just unit testing. There are obvious disadvantages to working with a separate testing team. Most importantly, if testing uncovers an area requiring rework, to what timebox can the rework be assigned? There just should not be the slack in the plan to allow this sort of activity to be accommodated – unless, of course, the timeboxing approach is diluted. By all means, a large project can have a team of 'flying testers' who are pulled into timebox teams to see that tests are adequately carried out, but this should not be done after it has been agreed that a deliverable meets the quality criteria set at the beginning of the timebox.

Each team should have the technical and business skills necessary to perform the core of what they need to do. There may be the need for additional specialists to be called in as required. The testing specialists in the previous paragraph are an example. There are many others. For instance, having a reuse broker could be very useful if the organisation has its reuse strategy well organised. Another useful external expert could be a human computer integration specialist to ensure that the user interface is designed for maximum productivity, ease of use, etc. as well as looking at the wider issues concerning the operational environment. The support from specialists will depend on the nature of the project and the skills of the core teams.

If the project is using a development tool for the first time, it is advisable to have technical support for the team arranged before they start work. It is often the case that DSDM projects introduce new technology alongside the new process. Some such projects have had near disasters through not being able to make the tool behave in the way that they thought it should and through having poor support from the tool suppliers. However, do let the developers learn.

One project very sensibly trained all the developers in the new tool that they were going to use and brought in an expert to support them as they enhanced their knowledge throughout the project. Unfortunately, his productivity was ten times greater than that of any one else, so they let him do major parts of the development. Consequently, he had limited time available to solve the problems that arose among the novices. This was not a strategy to make future projects in that organisation work more effectively with the new tool.

It is extremely valuable to have an external facilitator for running JAD workshops (see Chapter 6). When the person running a JAD workshop has a vested interest in the way that the project is going, it can be very difficult for the workshop to gain the consensus that is needed. I have seen project managers going into

JAD sessions with a list of objectives that included 'Get the users to agree to X'. This is against the whole ethos of DSDM. It could be that X is not what is needed. An impartial facilitator will more easily uncover that Y is the solution and will gain agreement to it. The arguments put against using facilitators who are external to the project is that they cannot know all the details of the project. It is true that they cannot. However, the very best example that I have seen of a facilitator at work was getting a room full of about 60 people to agree to a way forward on a topic about which the facilitator had absolutely no knowledge of at all – in under two hours. Achieving consensus from 60 people in such a short time is dramatic enough – add to that the fact that the discussion was completely outside the facilitator's sphere of knowledge, and I hope the example will convince the sceptics that having a trained facilitator is more important than using someone with detailed project knowledge.

5.5 Monitoring progress

Once the project manager who is new to DSDM understands how to plan the activities of the project and what the team should look like, the next major area of concern is how to make sure that everything is working out. The key point to remember is that time is not the issue here. There is little point in asking a team member 'How much longer is this going to take?' because the answer is supplied by the end of the timebox in which he or she is working. What needs to be monitored is how much of the minimum usable subset is being achieved, that is how many of the 'must haves' have been satisfied at any one time.

The main tool for deciding on progress is the prioritised requirements rather than a Gantt chart of activities. The Gantt chart will show the timeboxes and the personnel associated with each timebox, but the supplementary documentation about what is to be produced in each timebox is far more important for control and monitoring purposes and is product based rather than activity based.

For high-level project information, the prime method of monitoring and reporting progress against the requirements is through the satisfactory completion of timeboxes. If timeboxes are given clear objectives and methods of demonstrating achievement of those objectives, there is nothing better than the end of timebox documentation to show that progress is being made. This is also easily understood by high-level management as evidence of progress. Additionally, the users in the team provide an informal channel to their own management and the wider user population for progress reporting and monitoring. The ambassador users will be fully aware of the progress being made both as they sign off the deliverables from timeboxes and as they participate in the ongoing activities within the timeboxes.

For more detailed, working-level monitoring and control, the best mechanism has been found to be a daily meeting of all the team. This should be short and sharp and held either at the beginning of the working day or at the end. Typically, these meetings last half an hour – sometimes they can be as short as ten minutes but never more than half an hour, unless a major issue needs to be discussed. The meetings are more effective than the project manager asking each individual how work is progressing, since areas of common concern can be identified by other team members. As a bonus, they supply the equivalent of 'standing by the coffee machine' to get good ideas from other people. There can be times when the team members feel that these meetings are a waste of time and that they should be getting on with the job, but project managers should stick to their guns and hold the meetings anyway.

The RAD section at British Airways has a very useful rule to be applied at their daily meetings. Nobody is allowed to say 'I am doing this task at the moment'. They have to say 'I have done this task' – however small. The rule has two advantages. Firstly, the project manager is getting real evidence of progress. Secondly, nobody likes to come to a meeting at which they are unable to report success when everybody else has. The result of the second point is that each team member is continually striving to have achieved something. This keeps the momentum of the project going. If someone turns up at the meeting with nothing to report, then there is probably an issue for the project manager to address.

5.6   Workload

A frequent concern of project managers is that they will have to ask the team to work overtime regularly. If the project has been properly estimated and risk avoidance strategies put in place, this should not be the norm. I know of several organisations in which the culture is to arrive as late as possible in the morning or to leave as early as possible in the evening. This will not work in a RAD environment. A full working day is necessary. The day is far more concentrated than most staff are used to and, as with all time-critical activity, there will be occasions when you have to call on the team to work longer than usual. However, as one project manager said to me 'You warned me against burn-out and said that the team should be given something more restful to do after a DSDM project. What you didn't say is that they wouldn't go back to more traditional working'. Longer hours do not mean more productive work is achieved, but developers enjoy DSDM projects so much that they will want to work longer – to satisfy their professional pride as much as anything else.

It is not only the developers who will be working in a more concentrated way. If the organisation is used to having project managers manage several projects at once, the scope of their responsibility will have to be drastically reduced. Even a very small DSDM project can be a full-time job for the project manager. Every day there are more things that need the project manager's attention because of the speed with which products are delivered. Any problem that arises must be dealt with immediately. Another project manager said that he would normally be able to manage five projects of a similar size to his current DSDM project, which kept him busy 100% of the time.

5.7 Key points

■ Project planning is based around the timebox.

■ Functional and non-functional requirements should be grouped and allocated to timeboxes.

■ The contingency in timeboxes is contained in the lower priority requirements that may not be satisfied.

■ Estimating the length of timeboxes should involve the team.

■ DSDM defines roles and responsibilities for both users and developers.

■ Key roles that are DSDM-specific include:

  1. The visionary (a senior user) to ensure the overall business objectives are adhered to.

  2. The ambassador user who brings business knowledge into the team on a day-to-day basis throughout the project.

  3. The technical coordinator who ensures that all work fits into the system architecture and meets the required technical standard.

■ DSDM teams should be no more than six people, including the ambassador user(s).

■ Progress should be monitored daily.

■ The concentration of work for all concerned is greater than on traditional projects.

CHAPTER SIX

Impact on the organisation

Making decisions

The major impact on many organisations that implement DSDM is in the way that decisions are made about the direction that a project takes. Such decisions are made throughout the life of a project, and they have to be made very quickly indeed if the project is not to falter. For the decision-making processes to operate speedily, DSDM's second principle of empowerment of the team should be rigorously applied.

If the culture of the IT solution provider is to allow only major decisions to be made by a project board (or a similar body), then DSDM will significantly increase the demands on the project board's time. DSDM projects that have worked within such an environment have found that one or two members of the board have had to be contacted for decisions several times a week. This is obviously not ideal as, at best, it affects the working day of important people within the organisation or, at worst, delays decisions because those people have other tasks to carry out for the good of the organisation.

If the culture does demand the use of project boards, the board members should have their responsibilities clearly defined. This is normal practice, but the 'standard' responsibilities should be assessed for their validity in DSDM. It is a common complaint of board members of early DSDM projects in an organisation that, if the team is empowered, then they do not have any authority. Involving them effectively is as necessary as involving the Ambassador Users in the team. So what does a project board do in a DSDM project? Board members have responsibility for finance and are called in if significant changes to the original plan are envisaged. The Ambassador Users are making decisions on a daily basis. They are accepting work as it is produced rather than a few weeks later at a formal project board meeting. Only the team should make decisions at the day-to-day level, and the project board should be confident that such decisions do not affect the cost of the project or the proposed business benefits detrimentally. Frequent reports from the project manager will build that confidence. The frequency of reports will depend on the speed with which the project is operating, but they will probably be produced every one or two weeks. A simple one-page status report should suffice.

A strongly hierarchical organisation in which people work within well-defined grades or ranks can make it very difficult for the 'lower orders' to take responsibility for the decisions that they are required to make during a project. In this sort of organisation, the Ambassador User will probably not come from high enough up the organisation to have been allowed to make decisions in the past. Such an Ambassador User can feel very unsure of where the limits of their responsibility lie. It can initially be very frightening for someone of this kind to feel that their decisions must be accepted by those higher up in the organisation. Often, they are right to feel unsure. For instance, in a military organisation, a non-commissioned officer will feel that what a senior officer has to say at a later date will necessarily carry more weight than their point of view now. Terms of reference must be given to the users operating within a hierarchical organisation. These should clearly state where the limits of decision-making lie. Terms of reference are useful anyway, but they are probably more important in this sort of organisation.

In several instances, empowerment has been given lip service only. The team are assured by all relevant senior staff that their decisions will be accepted, but when it comes to the crunch, this is not the case. Some senior managers are very reluctant to delegate responsibility to their staff. For some reason or other, this appears to be particularly true of IT management. They are more than happy for the business members of the team to be empowered but are firmly against empowering their own staff. The only way that delegation by senior staff can be improved is through education. Such education could be by running a one-day DSDM awareness course, but really senior staff may not feel able to attend. Another route is to have a RAD expert spend an hour or two explaining to senior members of staff the advantages to be gained from loosening the reins a little.

How decision-making at the team level is made to work will depend on the organisation concerned. I have provided just a few pointers here. The basic requirement is to trust the people who have been assigned to perform a particular role and for others to be sure that the trust is well founded. As stated in the ninth principle, collaboration and cooperation between all stakeholders is essential.

6.2 User involvement

The second major impact on the organisation results from releasing staff from their usual work to supply the necessary time to the project. The level of involvement should be as high as possible without seriously affecting the work of the business area in which the users normally reside.

The problem is that the users who will participate as Ambassador Users will usually be key staff within their area. If it is easy to get the time from an individual, then that person is probably not the one the project needs. This is a real 'Catch 22' situation. DSDM advocates full-time involvement in the project but, in the lean organisations of today, this is very often impossible. The important thing is to get a continual flow of information and feedback from the user community throughout the project.

The right people for the project are those individuals whose decisions will be respected by the rest of the user population and who have sufficient business knowledge to see 'the wider picture' wherever possible. Someone who is to represent a user community should be able to do just that. They should not be focused on the minutiae of their own work at the cost of other users' needs. If we were to produce a workflow system for a telemarketing department, the ideal Ambassador User is a supervisor. A telesalesperson may be too focused on the way the job is done now. The supervisor's manager is probably too divorced from the detail of what has to be done by the sales staff. On the other hand, the supervisor will have good knowledge of their daily work and should have a broader view of the department's operation than they do. The Ambassador User will report regularly to the other end users so their points of view will be captured, but it is important that the day-to-day decisions are made by someone with the correct breadth and depth of knowledge.

Our supervisor is essential to the running of the department, but she is also essential to the project. A compromise has to be reached. Given that a RAD project will not be of long duration (unless it faces years of incremental development), it is possible to get key business staff into the team, but usually through some sort of 'contract' for their time. Some real project examples follow.

One project had identified a very senior engineer as the Ambassador User. He was already working very long hours and could not afford to give up any of his day to the project. He made a contract with the development to arrive at work an hour earlier than his and their normal start time. Another project was building a system for city traders. Traders cannot afford to lose any of their working day, because time really is money in their business. So, the Ambassador Users on that project spent time with the developers after business had closed for the day. Yet another project was building a system for a part of the Civil Service that had faced stringent cutbacks in staff. There was absolutely no fat in the organisation at all. The solution for one of the Ambassador Users was to make time available from 09.00 to 10.30 on Monday, Wednesday and Friday. If the development team did not request his presence by 09.10, the time would be used for the Ambassador User's normal work.

The problems of getting a sufficient level of involvement from the right users are compounded when there is a very large user population. This is made even worse when a new system will affect a population that spans all levels of an organisation. Very careful classification of all the users needs to be made to ensure that all relevant views will be available to the project. It may mean that to have total representation requires having a group of Ambassador Users who significantly outnumber the developers. This will not work. In addition to the minimum possible number of users to participate in development, the project should set up a user panel who have frequent visibility of what is going on inside the development. One project that covered several regional centres within a very large organisation had a user panel that met every Friday at a location that all could reach within three hours.

When the system is for implementation across national boundaries, then e-mail, video-conferencing, etc. are ways of involving the users, but they are not the only solution. There should still be someone physically in contact with the team – rather than virtually. One example of building in the right level of user contact is contained in the Sysdeco case study. The developers were based in Cambridge, UK, but the customer was the *Boston Globe* in America. They worked the other way round. The team put an 'ambassador developer' into the *Boston Globe*. He carried out the front-line analysis work with the users and, through the use of e-mail, he could demonstrate the latest work of the development team. While the software was being demonstrated, he would have 'control' of development and would be able to make changes that were then sent back to the UK.

Essentially, if it is not worth the users giving up time from their normal jobs, the user management should consider whether or not the project is really worth doing. If it is, then there is usually a way of getting DSDM to work in the way it should. Perhaps the Sysdeco example is the most imaginative.

6.3   Better communication

DSDM speeds up the development process through shortening the communication lines between all parties involved. There are various ways in which this is achieved, but the prime objective is to make sure that the barriers that can stand between users and developers are just not present.

One major barrier that often exists is the barrier of language in the documents that are produced by IT for users to read and sign off. By bringing users into the team, so that they can visualise more easily what IT is doing for them, eliminates the need for many documents. It is far easier to question the meaning of something when the person is speaking to you than when a document arrives on your desk without sufficient explanation of some of the more jargon-ridden parts.

Another barrier is that large project teams must use formal, documented communications to be sure that everyone is aware of what is going on. The production of these documents can be time consuming and will, therefore, necessarily delay the transfer of information from the writer to the intended audience. By using small teams, a DSDM project can rely more heavily on informal communication, which can be faster and more efficient in ensuring that everyone knows the current status of the project activities and of its deliverables.

An effective small team will usually be more creative, particularly if as many viewpoints as possible are contained within the team. DSDM ensures that the key IT roles are present throughout the project rather than that the relevant business views are easily accessible. Collocating developers and users, wherever possible, shortens the communication lines between the business and IT. It is far easier to ask a question of somebody if they are nearby than when they are at the end of a phone line.

6.4   Joint application design (JAD) workshops

Bringing people together who have the right knowledge to avoid misunderstandings is the foundation of the whole approach. A very useful method of bringing such people together is through joint application design (JAD) workshops. Rush (1985) said that workshops for capturing requirements can take about one-fifth of the elapsed time of traditional techniques. Without having any metrics to support it, my view is that this is a conservative estimate of the saving in elapsed time. Perhaps this is because of the more sophisticated technology that is widely available to speed up the production of documents arising during workshops.

There is a great deal of literature and advice available on how to run JAD workshops and the topic is also covered in the *DSDM Manual*, so I will not deal with them here in detail except to talk about the use of JAD in DSDM. Martin (1991) divides up the workshops into joint requirements planning (JRP) for capturing the business requirements and JAD for the later technical workshops. Since the process is the same and it is just the content that differs, DSDM takes JAD to stand for joint application development. Hence, in DSDM, a JAD workshop can be at any point in the development process from project inception to delivery, wherever it would be useful.

The aims of a JAD workshop are to produce something and to achieve consensus among the participants as to the content of that thing. It is particularly useful in the business study, when the foundations of the project are being built. If one area of the business is to have its requirements placed at a lower level than another's, JAD workshops will enable that sort of decision to be made without rancour. The first phase in DSDM at which they are beneficial could be during the feasibility phase. This depends on the number of decision-makers that should be involved. Even before the project is under way, a strategy workshop to decide on a programme of projects and what needs to be done by when can be very useful indeed.

During the business study, JAD workshops are an excellent vehicle for obtaining an understanding of the processes to be supported and potentially automated, together with their information needs. How the processes are modelled will depend on the techniques that the organisation finds most useful. The RAD team in Norwich Union use pictorial views of the components of the system that are readily understood by the business participants in the workshop. A letter will be a picture of a letter; a role will be a picture of a person. These are similar to the rich pictures in soft systems analysis. Other organisations use business object models, data flow diagrams or swim diagrams to show the flow of information and the transfer of authority between different business components. Use what you know and what you think the workshop participants will understand. Concerns about using technical modelling techniques are unfounded. If a model is being built up in front of the users, it is very easy to explain the syntax as you go along.

Workshops can achieve the seemingly impossible. I ran a JAD workshop for an organisation that had a set of discrete systems, which it wanted to integrate for better information flow between the various departments. The workshop was attended by each of the department heads. We put together a corporate data model from scratch in about half a day. Admittedly, it was in need of later refinement, but it gave us sufficient information to understand most of the information needs of the organisation.

Later on in the process, JAD workshops can be used for prototyping the user interface. Again, depending on the technology support you wish to use, this can be through the use of anything from whiteboards or Post-its on flipcharts to fully automated screens.

It is important to decide what the workshop is for and whether it is valuable to take business participants away from their normal work. Data Sciences use JAD workshops for a multitude of activities both inside and outside DSDM, including business vision analysis, business process re-engineering, information systems strategy study, benefits analysis, requirements definition, technical systems options, acceptance test planning, service level agreements and team building. This is not an exhaustive list, but it should trigger ideas about when JAD can be used effectively. For the purposes of DSDM, it is worth picking out the combination of benefits analysis and requirements definition. It is often hard to decide on the priorities of the system. If benefits analysis has been carried out before the definition and prioritisation of requirements, such decisions can be far easier to make and, in some instances, can make themselves. ICL Peritas has used JAD for other activities, such as determining the content and logistics of a training programme for a very large user population, and change management to encourage new ways of working after installation of the new system.

6.5 Training users

For user involvement to be successful, it is advisable that all parties who will be involved in the project are fully aware of their roles and responsibilities in DSDM. This can best be achieved by running a DSDM awareness course. The value of setting aside one day for training at the start of the project cannot be underestimated. It brings to their attention many of the issues which might otherwise remain in doubt.

Two examples from DSDM projects can illustrate the need for training. In one project, the awareness day completely changed the attitude of a key user who had been 'bitten' by IT once too often. At the beginning of the day, he did not understand the level of influence that he would have throughout the project and was opposed to the idea of a new system. By the end of the day, he saw that he might get what he really needed this time. The system has now been delivered and he is a real champion of everything that it does. On another project, it was the user management who had their attitude changed. They had been told by the IT department that a branch supervisor would be needed to work with them for three days a week throughout the project. They had agreed to this, but it was not until the awareness course that they saw why it was necessary. Indeed, one manager said at the end of the session 'They really mean it!'. The comment suggests that the user management would not have been wholehearted in their support of the DSDM approach. Without the awareness days, both of these projects would probably not have achieved the necessary user involvement, or at best the user involvement would have been only on sufferance.

6.6   Key points

- Decisions that are not in the control of the immediate project team must be made very quickly.

- The continuous involvement of Ambassador Users is essential to the success of DSDM.

- Ambassador users must have sound business knowledge and should be respected by their colleagues, at all levels.

- 'Contracts' for their time should be agreed at the outset and adhered to.

- DSDM shortens communication channels between all parties, both inside and outside the team.

- JAD workshops are a powerful means of achieving this.

- It is advisable to train all the users who will be involved in the project, so that they understand their roles and responsibilities.

CHAPTER SEVEN

Never mind the quality?

'Good enough' software

The main aim of DSDM as a method is to remove the 'quick and dirty' image of RAD. This is achieved through a strong focus on delivering what is needed, when it is needed, while ensuring an agreed level of maintainability is built into the software and its supporting documentation.

Traditionally, quality-related activities have striven to drive out all identified defects before delivery. Much of the work of quality assurance and control is aimed at ensuring as low a defect rate as possible. Such an aim may not be possible in the time-scales of a DSDM project. That does not mean that developers are delivering unusable software that crashes every day or that requires the users to save their work every few minutes in fear of loss of data at the desktop before it is sent to the database. What it means is that a certain level of imperfection is acceptable. Software has to be 'good enough' – and no more or less. Defining what is good enough is often difficult and requires an element of pragmatism. However, if the business agrees that the functionality in the minimum usable subset has been provided adequately and the IT staff are happy that they are not going to be called in regularly to fix the non-business aspects of the system, then the system can be accepted. To achieve acceptance of the delivered system, it may be necessary to disable a malfunctioning item and postpone its delivery to a later date. It is permissible to do this only if the component is not part of the minimum usable subset that must be delivered.

All of the above means that a different approach to quality-related activities may be needed by an organisation that is introducing DSDM.

7.2 Building in quality

One of the areas in which a definite line must be taken by the members of a RAD team is the level of maintainability that the system will demonstrate. DSDM defines three possible levels of maintainability and the one to be achieved on the project must be agreed during the business study, as it will drive the quality control activities for the rest of the project. The three levels are:

- the system must be maintainable from its first delivery into the operational environment;
- initially, maintainability is not guaranteed, but will be addressed after delivery;
- the system is a short-term fix and, therefore, will not be maintainable and the developers reserve the right to remove the system from production once it has served its immediate purpose.

The first level is obviously the most time consuming in the initial development and will demand excellent quality controls during all stages of development. However, the chances are that it will provide savings over the life of the system. The second level will deliver the first increment of the system faster but may be more costly in the long term, since doing the same work in two passes will incur more overheads in implementation, etc.

If the second option is chosen, two things should be borne in mind. Firstly, that even though maintainability is not an immediate issue, the future rebuilding should be remembered at all times in order to make the rework less troublesome. Records should be kept of parts that have been skimped with respect to maintainability. Secondly, the project must be sure that future funding is guaranteed to be available. If not, the use of the second level of maintainability should be seriously reconsidered. The maintenance staff will not want to take over a system that will be difficult for them to understand – even though that is what is asked of them all the time!

The third level of maintainability is the hardest to achieve in practice but, if the user management has signed up to this approach, the suppliers must be determined in their efforts to take the system out of the production environment. It is essential that the system is removed at the time agreed. There are too many systems in operation that were built quickly to solve a specific problem and that remain in place causing endless headaches to IT departments as they try to keep them running effectively.

7.3 | Testing

IT management often worry that testing will be squeezed out as RAD projects race to deliver. One of the principles of DSDM is that testing happens throughout the lifecycle and is not something that happens at the end – after all the decisions have been made about the content of the software. Timeboxes are the mechanism through which testing is a continuous activity throughout the development process.

Within a timebox, testing is performed simultaneously at several levels, from unit testing through integration and system testing to acceptance testing – not forgetting regression testing – which is particularly vital in an iterative approach to development. Paul Herzlich, who wrote the testing chapter in the *Manual*, calls this a 'broadband' approach to testing.

Unit testing is very similar to that carried out by developers in traditional projects. Additionally, if a component can be seen or exercised by a user in the team, then it is. This brings the element of third-party testing into the timebox. It is dangerous to pass the testing to a third party who is outside the constraints of the timebox. They may not have the same focus on the relative priorities of the timebox in terms of deliverables, quality criteria and time-scale.

Integration testing also happens within a timebox, if its software deliverables need to be integrated with a software deliverable from a preceding timebox. In this way, integration testing happens incrementally throughout development. Indeed, as development in timeboxes progresses, the number of components to be integrated will move towards the number in the system to be delivered. Hence, the integration testing will move away from technical concerns about interfaces to concerns about integrated functionality. As the number of components increases, and as the components mature towards their target functionality, integration testing shifts in focus from technical integration of low-level interfaces to testing of the combined functionality of the overall product. In other words, it moves towards system testing.

At no time should a software component be delivered by the team without undergoing unit and user testing at the very least.

The presence of users in the team puts an early emphasis on validation, as opposed to verification, which is the traditional mode of testing in the early stages. In other words, early on in the project, the users are looking forward to the viability of the system in use rather than the developers focusing entirely on whether or not their code fits with previously defined specifications. This brings down the cost of fixing the sort of errors that are often discovered during the traditional user acceptance test at the end of a project or, worse, when the system is in production.

A perennial problem in user acceptance testing is that users do not understand how to produce test scripts. As Ambassador Users see how developers handle the testing of technical aspects of the system, they become increasingly competent in user testing. The Ambassador Users are, therefore, ideal staff for putting together formal acceptance tests by the wider user population when they are needed.

The overall effect of this approach is that often more time is spent in testing than would be considered the norm. If the testing techniques used are appropriate and focused on finding errors rather than proving that something works as specified, the result should be a system that can be trusted in the operational environment.

An overall strategy for testing should be defined before any software is produced. This should cover everything from unit testing to acceptance testing. It is not possible to delay the strategy until later, or the work of timeboxes may be invalidated instead of building confidence in the system as it is developed.

On large projects or because of contractual constraints placed on external systems providers, it may be necessary to cater for testing activities that are not contained within a specific timebox. If the strategy of testing as much as possible as you go is adhered to, the time for these activities should be minimal. There really should be no rework encountered, so the elapsed time should be just for running the tests, which is the least of a tester's worries during activities like contractual acceptance testing. If rework is required, then the organisation should look at its testing strategy and try to improve things on the next project.

Now for a bit of motherhood and apple pie! Many developers learn testing informally and are often surprised when told of the various approaches to choosing test cases. It is advisable, if testing is to work effectively, that at least one member of a timebox team has undergone formal training in testing.

7.4 DSDM and TickIT

The TickIT scheme in the UK provides rigorous certification and third-party auditing procedures around the ISO 9001 standard, together with the ISO 9000–3 notes for guidance for software development. TickIT has been so successful in the UK marketplace that it is moving to international usage. No large software house in the UK can hope to stay in operation without TickIT certification. The introduction of DSDM and its increased usage have caused some concern to the TickIT auditing companies, since many see RAD as a 'licence to hack' – completely contrary to all that TickIT stands for. However, as one large software supplier after another espoused the use of DSDM, it became obvious that such organisations would not want to jeopardise their reputations for delivering quality software and that there was something of value in DSDM for quality-conscious organisations.

The result is that the British Standards Institution has produced (with assistance from the DSDM Consortium) a specific guide for the application and assessment of DSDM in a TickIT environment. There is nothing in the guide (Woodhead *et al.*, 1997), *Dynamic Systems Development Method and TickIT,* that differs from the *DSDM Manual.* It simply extracts and documents the procedures and controls to which the customer and supplier should conform and that the third-party TickIT auditor of DSDM projects should expect to see in place. None of these are in contradiction of the contents of the international standards, but the document provides a useful abstraction and collation of the many aspects of quality management that are buried in the text of the *DSDM Manual.*

7.5 New procedures for old

The standards in an organisation that relate to the quality of products will remain unchanged, but the standards relating to how that quality is achieved will probably have to change. Many existing quality management systems are firmly based on the waterfall lifecycle. They assume that there will be a detailed statement of requirements and a functional specification against which all deliverables will be assessed. As a result, the quality control procedures are focused on achieving satisfactory compliance with these documents. In DSDM, some software may be delivered before the requirements are documented for the full system, and the functional specification is a much smaller document that also grows incrementally with the software. In fact, the Functional Model that replaces the functional specification is ahead of the software but, in many instances, only by a matter of weeks, and cannot really be used as an instrument for change control.

Change control is one of the areas most likely to be affected by the introduction of DSDM. This brings with it the need to reconsider the standard contractual arrangements with external suppliers or the basis of agreement as to what will be delivered by internal suppliers. For external suppliers, it is preferable not to choose a fixed price approach, as it often requires a detailed specification before design and development work can proceed. A more flexible approach is needed. Fixed price can be used, but the basis for acceptance probably has to be changed. For instance, some external suppliers use the number of function points delivered as the basis for acceptance, rather than complying with a document that is liable to change until very late in the project. There are several approaches in use, but all of them require some change to the way contractual agreement can be achieved.

Another area in which standard procedures will probably need to change is in the area of testing. Section 7.3 discussed the move away from the V-model of testing, in which testing activity is related to the development stages in the waterfall lifecycle. If the testing procedures are based on this approach, then they will need to be reconsidered. DSDM does not allow for discrete stages of testing. This is largely because, instead of one big V-model for the project, there are a multiplicity of little V-models applied throughout development as timeboxes (or groups of timeboxes) take a tranche of requirements through to coding (Figure 7.1).

Testing activities will be just as formal as usual, but they may not be as formally documented prior to testing taking place. There is very little point in producing a test specification, if the component to be tested is not produced. This reason alone will mean that procedures for testing may have to change. It is perfectly acceptable to define early on what the test will demonstrate and to document what the test actually does at the time it is carried out. Capture and replay tools are particularly useful in lessening the burden of testing documentation. As always, a log of test successes and failures should be kept to demonstrate the progress towards completion of testing.

To ensure auditability of the process and products, internal auditors should be involved in any changes to the procedures and in initial quality and project planning activities until an organisation has 'bedded down' in the application of DSDM. Where auditors who are external to the organisation are involved, they too should be consulted if at all possible. They are stakeholders in the process and should be treated as Adviser Users.

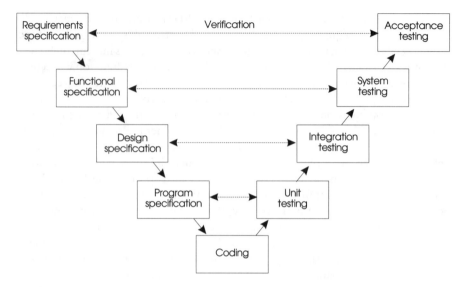

Figure 7.1   The V-model showing which testing activities verify which specifications.

7.6 **The capability maturity model**

The capability maturity model (CMM), developed by the Software Engineering Institute (SEI) at Carnegie Mellon University in the United States, is the most common model for software process maturity. It encompasses the process management and quality principles into five levels, where every level has a number of key practices associated with it. Following is the main characterisation of the CMM process maturity levels and the impact of adopting DSDM for organisations at these different levels of maturity.

1. **The initial level** where the software process is characterised as *ad hoc*, and occasionally chaotic. Few processes are defined, and success depends on individual effort.
2. **The repeatable level** where basic management processes are established to track cost, schedule and functionality. The necessary process discipline is in place to repeat earlier successes on projects with similar applications.
3. **The defined level** where the software process is characterised as standard and consistent. At this level, the software process for both management and engineering activities is documented, standardised and integrated into an organisation-wide software process. All projects use a documented and approved version of the organisation's process for developing and maintaining software.
4. **The managed level** where the software process is characterised as predictable. At this level, detailed measures of the software process and product

quality are collected. Both the software process and the products are quantitatively understood and controlled using detailed measures.

5. **The optimising level** where the software process is characterised as continuously improving. At this level, continuous process improvement is enabled by quantitative feedback from the process and from testing innovative ideas and technologies.

Most organisations are at level 1 of the CMM. The DSDM Consortium believes that introducing DSDM into an organisation can help the organisation achieve process maturity level 2. Successful adoption of DSDM will inject a degree of process discipline into the organisation and progress the process maturity of the organisation to the CMM level 2 or above. This is the level where a disciplined process is in place. (It is also the level where ISO 9001 operates at its most basic level of process maturity.) Once DSDM is established as a practice, the organisation can aspire to improving its software processes to achieve higher levels of maturity. DSDM will help establish the main key process areas required for establishing a disciplined process. The mapping between level 2 of the CMM and DSDM covers all the key process areas specified by the CMM for level 2 as follows:

■ requirements management, which is achieved through the Ambassador User role in the DSDM team;
■ software project planning;
■ software project tracking and oversight;
■ software configuration management, which is a key feature of DSDM;
■ software quality assurance;
■ subcontract management, which is mentioned briefly in this chapter, but covered in more depth in the *DSDM Manual.*

7.7 Key points

■ The focus is on building software that is sufficiently robust to be usable – and no more than that.

■ DSDM builds quality controls into the process.

■ Maintainability objectives should be agreed during the business study.

■ Testing is earlier in the lifecycle than traditionally and incorporates all classes of testing from very early on.

■ Introducing DSDM into an organisation will probably mean that quality control and assurance procedures will have to change.

■ DSDM fits well with both ISO 9000–3 and the CMM.

CHAPTER EIGHT

The RAD professional

8.1 'No more quick and dirty'

Over the last few years, RAD developers have acquired a bad name for putting systems together without regard to the long-term enhancement and amendments that will be necessary. Many of the RAD developers who did not conform to this image pretended that they were not doing RAD at all. DSDM has allowed these more professional IT staff to come out of the closet. They are now able to say that they are using DSDM, a recognised method. One member of the Consortium said that previously his team had been nicknamed 'the seagulls', because they swooped down to pick the choicest IT developments and left a mess behind. Now, they are respected and seen as being at the leading edge.

Additionally, IT staff can be certified as DSDM practitioners through a rigorous examination procedure. To qualify for this status, RAD staff must attend an accredited DSDM course, have demonstrated at least six months of RAD work, have written a paper about a RAD project in which they have participated and undergone an oral examination to test their detailed understanding of DSDM. By demanding not only training, but experience and demonstrable understanding of the issues within RAD, the DSDM practitioner certificate is seen to be of value within the UK, and it is expected that, as DSDM grows internationally, RAD developers and project managers everywhere will see the certificate as a means of demonstrating professionalism in a field that many view as just a means of cutting corners. Part Three contains more information about training and certification.

A word of warning. It has come to the attention of the DSDM training and accreditation work group that attendance at a DSDM practitioner course is being claimed as conferring practitioner status. This is probably through misunderstanding of the rules, but organisations thinking of employing DSDM practitioners should ask to see the certificate that will have been issued jointly by the DSDM Consortium and the country's examining body (e.g. the Information Systems Examination Board in the UK). Any other certificate is simply proof of course attendance issued by a training provider as the first step towards certification.

8.2   Skills and attributes

Whatever the methods used, almost every project that has failed has done so because of some issue related to the people involved. It is rarely the technology that creates the real problems; technological problems are hard but are often more tractable than those relating to people. One could almost say that IT personnel thrive on technological problems, but they often find the softer issues more difficult to resolve.

RAD developers must not only be skilled in the technology they use, but they should also be effective communicators who are responsive to the needs of the users in their team. Many developers are very focused on the technology and the improvement of their own technical skills to the detriment of their soft skills. Indeed, some IT staff should never be let near people outside their own domain. We have all met somebody in IT who is a genius at what they do but who is unable to interact effectively with other people. Every member of a DSDM team must be able to work in a cooperative and collaborative way with all other members of the team.

Moreover, owing to the small team structures in DSDM, there should be no clear delineation between the various IT roles. The DSDM developer will have a broader view than just analysis or design or programming. For instance, someone whose main skills are in programming must be able to see beyond the programming task to understanding the users' requirements and interpreting them into a computerised form. This means that they should be capable of some analysis and design, but will obviously require support from other members of the team as they increase their skill set. The DSDM team should contain all the necessary core skills for a project, and some members will be stronger in one area than another. By working collaboratively, every developer's skills are strengthened by the presence of others.

All of the above can be summed up in the statement that nobody should be protective of their area of work or the products arising from it. DSDM developers should actively promote user comments. Nevertheless, it can be disheartening to show work to a user who then pulls it to pieces because it does not do what was asked for. The ability for developers to change their views quickly about what is required is essential in DSDM. Flexibility is the key. Some developers find the need for flexibility very threatening, while others flourish in the DSDM environment. The developer who is firmly embedded in a regimented way of working will not make a good RAD developer.

Several organisations worry about the move to DSDM. They feel that their IT staff who have always worked in hierarchically managed projects to clearly defined specifications will not be able to move to the flatter management style and more flexible specifications in DSDM. Admittedly, there are some developers who do not take to the new ways of working, but in the many DSDM projects that have been undertaken by organisations used to more traditional approaches, there have been very few developers who have not made the transition. Some have taken to it immediately and others have taken a few months to acclimatise themselves. In the projects that I have come into contact with or have heard reports about, only a handful of developers have felt uncomfortable in the long run. The stumbling block for these individuals has usually been the customer contact. They have found it hard to have their prototypes rejected by users who are seen as being unable to make up their minds. These 'failures' usually exhibit the rigorous, logical thinking that is necessary in IT to a very high degree and expect to see it in everyone they deal with.

8.3 Self-management

DSDM is a controlled process, but it does leave a lot of the controls to the individual team members to perform. For instance, the guidelines on configuration management provide a set of rules for the project to follow, but how effective it is in practice will depend very much on the developers themselves. Hence, all the best practices that have grown within IT over the last few decades are still present, but they need to be seen as important by the individual rather than something that is imposed by IT management, the project manager or the quality management system.

Some DSDM projects are very small indeed with just one or two developers. Where this is the case, it is even more important that IT management can be sure that all the relevant controls are effectively applied. It can be very easy in such a small team to think that the controls in DSDM can be ignored. This is never the case: DSDM has defined the minimum to make the final system both usable and maintainable.

8.4 Key points

- DSDM is not a home for hackers.
- The practitioner certificate demonstrates professionalism in RAD.
- Developers should be 'team players' whose focus is not only on technological problems.
- DSDM practitioners should be quality conscious and manage their work effectively.

CHAPTER NINE

Prototyping is not a waste of time

9.1 Bridging the language barriers

DSDM is more than anything about improving communications between all parties involved in the development of a system. Prototyping is one of the ways that communication between the developers and the users is made more effective. Because of the technical nature of their work, IT personnel use a language that is adapted for their particular needs, as in any specialist discipline. To the layman, this language is obscure. Moreover, the users often have their own language, which relates to the business area in which they work. The users' jargon is usually less arcane than that of IT, but communicating across this language barrier has been a perennial problem.

The use of diagrammatic analysis and design techniques has gone some way towards alleviating the problem. Indeed, the use of diagrammatic techniques has evolved on the basis that a picture is worth a thousand words and a picture with syntactic rules is even better. Unfortunately, an interpreter is often needed for users to understand what the pictures mean, and the accompanying text is often a hindrance rather than a help. The basic problem is that static abstractions of the proposed system do not easily convey the dynamic nature of the system under construction. A dynamic, working model of the system or part of the system is far more effective in showing the thoughts of the developers than a document or set of documents. We could say that a working model is worth a thousand pictures.

A further problem is the limited attention paid to the user interface by many analysis and design methods. The increase in interactive methods of working over the last decade has made the design of the user interface one of the deciding factors as to whether or not a system will be considered of operational benefit or not. The user interface is seen by the end users as the way the system operates – whatever is happening underneath. It must match the way that users think and the way that their business functions.

While the layout and navigation around the user interface are obviously important, even something as simple as using the wrong word can create problems. For instance, in a system being put together for air traffic controllers, the developers used a 'Clear' button for clearing the screen. The air traffic controllers took this to mean that they were clearing the aircraft to land! Fortunately, the error was discovered during early prototyping. This is a powerful example of the misconceptions that the different languages can introduce.

9.2 But the users keep changing their minds!

The title of this section is a common complaint among IT staff. What is really happening is that, as a part of the system is demonstrated to them, the users become more aware of what is being developed and what the system can do for them. It is very difficult to explain in the abstract what is needed. Could you describe a new machine that you have never seen before without the technical knowledge of the components necessary for that machine to operate successfully?

Managed effectively, timeboxing will ensure that the changes that are asked for are necessary and relevant to the task in hand. Minor aspects, such as the colour of objects at the user interface, are immaterial and can be addressed later, if they are seen to be important by the larger user population. Also, when considering the minutiae of presentation, it should be borne in mind that the Ambassador Users are not always right. They are there to make sure that the system operates correctly and is easy for the users to operate. One user became so keen on the use of colour (having previously been using green screens) that she demanded red and green to demonstrate the different statuses of the information. This could have been disastrous for colour-blind staff. However, a change to the grouping and flow of information to fit the way that the user community thinks about it, or a request for different information to be displayed, is not evidence of change just for change's sake. It is the Ambassador User realising that things could be done better.

To ensure that the system is evolving in the right direction, it is a good idea to bring in different user views as often as possible. The Ambassador User provides the front line during prototyping but, when there is a key area being addressed, a demonstration should be given to the relevant Adviser Users. I am afraid that they may well ask for something to change, but it is better to find out early that a particular need has not been successfully addressed rather than later on when it will be more difficult to incorporate.

The objectives setting meeting at the start of a timebox should decide whether a wider user view is needed or not. The fact that time-scales are tight or that the developers feel the prototype may not be elegant enough for a wider audience should not be reasons for deciding against a demonstration to the adviser users. If the knowledge of the ambassador users needs to be supplemented, then it should be.

9.3 Categories of prototypes

DSDM uses the word, prototyping, because that is the industry 'standard', but they are not truly prototypes: they are partial system components. A DSDM prototype is not 'all done by mirrors', but is built using the platform on which all the development work is done, and meeting all the required standards. In other words, the prototypes are intended to be evolutionary rather than throw-away: they will evolve into the delivered system. Of course, there will be occasions when it is better to throw something away and start again, but the aim at all times should be to build on what is there already.

There are four categories of prototype recommended by DSDM that are used at different stages of development and have very different purposes. They are:

- **business** prototypes for demonstrating the business functions being built into the system;
- **usability** prototypes for investigating aspects of the user interface that do not affect the functionality;
- **performance and capacity** prototypes for ensuring that the system will be able to handle the workloads successfully;
- **capability/design** prototypes for trying out a particular design approach.

While the purpose of each prototype category is different, it will often be the case that some combination of them will be used. For instance, a common combination is the business and usability prototype, but this approach should not be taken as a matter of course. If the functionality is at all complex, it may be better to get it right before worrying about the presentation aspects. Conversely, if there is no standard for user interface design, it is a good idea to get some usability prototyping done first. The categories of prototype to be built into a timebox should be decided at its outset based on the aims of the timebox.

Because of their purpose of demonstrating functions, business prototypes are obviously produced during the functional modelling iteration.

The usability prototypes can be produced during both functional modelling and design and build, but their primary usage will be during functional modelling – to gain user buy-in as much as anything. Also, leaving usability issues until later in the lifecycle can adversely affect the overall design strategy.

Performance and capacity are clearly design-based prototypes and belong in the design and build iteration.

Capability/design prototypes are in the category that is most likely to be thrown away. They can be produced at any time. They are used to try out various design strategies or even a potential toolset, if a choice is available. They could be produced as early as feasibility to provide a proof of concept. They are potentially useful in the business study when the high-level system architecture is produced. However, their most usual position is during design and build to try out an alternative design, if the one that was originally envisaged is not working as well as expected. This is often very late in the project and, therefore, they are the least used category of prototype.

9.4 Getting effective feedback

How the various prototype categories are used will have an impact on how effective they are for their respective purposes. Time should be allowed for the users to consider what they are seeing and to comment. This is particularly true of the business prototypes, which are possibly rather fragile with large holes that make it difficult for the users to try out themselves. It is not uncommon for a developer to demonstrate a business prototype too quickly for the audience to think through all the ramifications of what is being presented. No adverse comments are forthcoming and the developer goes on to refine the work on an unsound basis. The result is that later, when the users see the next stage, they appear to have changed their minds from the earlier session. Prototyping is a dangerous way of developing systems, if the business knowledge of the users is not utilised to the full extent. Development just degenerates into coding before you know what you are supposed to be doing.

Usability prototypes should be given to the users to operate with as little steering as possible from the developers: they are not going to be able to sit beside all the users for all time. By leaving the users to operate the prototype themselves, important areas of misunderstanding will arise. It is very useful to get the users to talk through what they are doing and why they have chosen a particular action. This will help the developers to understand where they can improve the presentation, navigation, etc.

Concerns are often expressed about raising user expectations through early production of usability prototypes. One advantage of the usability prototype is that it may well fall over unexpectedly. Another way of keeping expectations within realistic terms is to make a prototype perform rather poorly by putting in wait states – as long as they are removed later. In fact, wait states are a good idea, as they can be used to slow a prototype down to its expected speed when in production, so avoiding potential disappointment later when the users compare the delivered system with what they used during development. This is especially important if a higher specification of machine is being used during development than the one available to most end users.

One of DSDM's products is the set of prototyping review documents. These are not produced after the event. If a prototype is being demonstrated, the demonstrator should be supported by a scribe who notes down all the points from the users as they are raised. If the users are trying out a prototype themselves, they should write down their own comments as they arise, but this approach should only be used if a large trial is being undertaken. The best approach is to have a developer sitting beside the user catching every comment as it is made. Every effort should be made to gain complimentary comments as well as the adverse ones. It is just as useful to know what should not be changed as what should. At the end of the session, the comments should be gone through with the users, and the relative importance of the comments noted as the basis for future development.

Users should have business scenarios that they work through when exercising any class of prototype. If these are not used, then the users can be so caught up in the prototype as to lose sight of what they are trying to assess. This is particularly true for users who are moving to a graphical user interface for the first time.

9.5 Keeping control

If a major change to the requirements (rather than a refinement) arises during the development of a prototype, it should be dealt with immediately through the channels prescribed by the project. All refinements to the requirements should be recorded as soon as possible after they have been identified and certainly no later than the end of the timebox in which the prototype is being produced.

The use of prototyping clarifies the business needs, but can muddy the technical vision if prototyping activities are not controlled within the technical framework. The technical vision is the responsibility of the Technical Coordinator. No prototype should be allowed to deviate from the design that is in place or to be non-conformant with the standards that have been set either by the organisation or by the project. Before any prototype is built, the Technical Coordinator should inform the prototype builders of any system constraints that will apply to the work they are about to undertake, and should remind them of its place in the overall system architecture. If the prototype builders identify a 'better' way of doing something, they should check with the Technical Coordinator that it does not endanger other areas of the architecture. When the prototype is nearly complete, its detailed design should be checked by the Technical Coordinator and incorporated into the system architecture. If technical issues arise during prototyping that cannot be addressed in the time-scale or are outside the remit of the prototype, they should be reported to the Technical Coordinator.

The use of the three-phase timebox of investigation, refinement and consolidation will stop developers from tinkering round the edges. With a clear set of priorities to work to, they will not try to 'gold-plate' the prototype. Their attention will be focused on delivering what is really needed rather than going down paths that they personally find interesting and challenging.

9.6 Key points

- The differences between the languages of the users and developers should not be underestimated.
- Prototyping helps to break down the language barriers. Prototypes provide a common language.
- It also ensures that the right system is being built – errors are trapped early in the process.
- DSDM prototypes evolve into the delivered system.
- Four categories of prototype are defined and are used in particular phases of development: business, usability, performance and capacity, and capability/design.
- Evaluation of prototypes through demonstration or user trials needs to be carefully managed to ensure all feedback from the users is captured.

continued over

Key points continued

- Developers need to be kept aware of the technical aspects of the system during prototyping. The technical coordinator role has an important part in ensuring that this happens.

CHAPTER TEN

Technology support

10.1 The need for technology support

Rapid application development has been made possible largely by recent developments in technology. The ability to visualise what the developers are thinking and to gain feedback from that visualisation is the basis of much of RAD. However, it is not the total answer. The technology support for a controlled RAD process does not lie solely in the easy generation of analysis and design models, screens and code. If the process is to be controlled, then strong emphasis should also be placed on automated support for the necessary controls. Controls are an overhead on productive work, albeit a necessary one. Savings in effort can be made by automating the control of the status of, and access to, work products and in ensuring that they have been created correctly.

RAD developers are like any other developers: they find certain activities tedious even though they see the necessity for them. They would much rather spend their time creating the solution than controlling it. Therefore, it is the control activities that are likely to be squeezed out of their schedules when they are under pressure to deliver. So, what do developers find most boring? Ask any group of developers and documentation is number one on the list. Hence, the ability to produce documentation 'at the press of a button' should be one of the elements of a RAD support environment. Another area that does not enthral developers is configuration management. However, configuration management is of prime importance in a RAD environment, where more things are being produced at a faster rate than in a traditional method. The need for support in this area is obviously fundamental. It should be easy for the developers to place their work under configuration management as soon as possible and as often as they should without causing them to slow down in their development activities. Testing also looms large as something that developers see as a necessary evil but which would be a much more productive activity with tool support. The list goes on.

10.2   DSDM support environments

The Consortium has a policy not to recommend specific tools. Many of our members are tool vendors and it would be invidious to compare one offering with another. Indeed, it would be an onerous and awesome task that is best left to organisations who specialise in providing impartial, third-party assessments of tools. However, some members have taken the messages in the *DSDM Manual* to heart and have moved or are moving their tools nearer to what is required by the method.

DSDM has defined a RAD tool 'nirvana' (Figure 10.1). It is an environment that will support the whole process from feasibility to implementation (including aspects such as reverse engineering for legacy code) with all the necessary controls as automated as possible. It does not exist and it is unlikely that any one tool vendor will offer the fully integrated set. Indeed, it is yet another cry for an integrated project support environment (IPSE), but one that is designed for RAD projects. Such an environment requires integration at a number of levels:

- **presentation** to provide a common 'look and feel' across all tools;
- **data** so that all tools share the same repository;
- **control** so that one tool can notify and/or initiate actions in other tools;
- **platform** in order to port the toolset from one platform to another.

Maybe such an environment will exist in the future but, in the meantime, we have to be more realistic and look for tools that will make savings in time and effort without being too costly. If we focus on the money side, several low-cost tools have been found to have beneficial impact on effort. Low-cost tools for code and schema generation are available, as are tools for prototype generation. Both of these speed up development markedly compared with coding by hand. Another

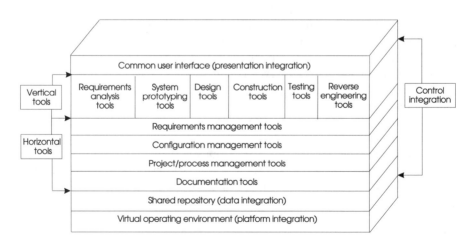

Figure 10. 1   An ideal support environment.

area where inexpensive tools can help is in the perennial headache of documentation. Automated support for creating documentation is readily available. Fortunately, many tools are self-documenting.

The ability to share information easily is also necessary. It can be of little value for one developer to produce an item, if it cannot easily be used by other members of the team. A repository is the solution to this. However, DSDM demands that it be a controlled repository. Developers performing different roles on a project should have different access rights to products and their variants and to products under construction. The access control should be automated to avoid abuse, whether intentional or otherwise.

10.3 Testing tools

One of the components of the DSDM support environment is testing tools. There are many varieties of testing tool available on the market and DSDM strongly advocates the use of tools in this area. Producing a tested system in a very short time can only be made easier with effective tools.

A very useful class of tools are capture and replay tools. These can lessen the need for documented test scripts. The quickest way to document tests is to record them as they are performed. A great deal of developer time can be saved through this route. Not only does this eliminate the need for producing 'paper' scripts before testing takes place, but the tests can be archived as evidence of which tests have taken place. Capture and replay tools are also extremely beneficial in building up regression test suites that can be left to run overnight while the developers have a well-earned rest.

Static code analysers can relieve the effort in code inspection and lessen the need for third-party verification that the code is to the required standard.

If the testing toolset is to be really complete, then dynamic analysis tools will perform tests in the background, while demonstrations of a part of the software are taking place. Dynamic analysis includes checking array bounds and detecting memory leakage, etc.: things that should be tested but that may be difficult to fit into the tight schedule of a project.

10.4 Configuration management tools

DSDM asks a lot of configuration management. Everything that is produced (analysis models, designs, data, software, tests, test results, etc.) should all be kept in step with one another so that it is relatively easy to move back to a known 'build' state whenever the development has gone down a blind alley. This requirement means that automated support is probably essential and that the automated support should allow for many versions and variants. Ideally, configuration management should be integrated into the tools used but this is rarely the case (pardon the pun). Anyway, given the diversity of products that are under development at any one time, it is probably asking too much to expect all the relevant tools being used in a project to be sufficiently integrated to have every product in step. This means that a specialist configuration management tool should definitely be on the shopping list of an organisation that is planning to take DSDM seriously. The ability to baseline everything on a daily basis is the ideal. So, the tool should not incur too much of an overhead in its use. There are several excellent configuration management tools available that will do the job perfectly satisfactorily, if the procedures governing their use are firmly in place.

10.5 Effective tool usage

Although there are excellent tools on the market, any tool is only as good as its users. They should not be relied upon as the whole answer. The developers should be confident that they know how to use them properly and that the tools are an asset rather than otherwise. The purchaser of a RAD tool environment should think carefully before buying. It is possible in early DSDM projects to live with what you already have. Indeed, it is probably preferable not to introduce too many new things at the same time. Once the developers are used to the process, they will soon see where tool support would be particularly beneficial in their working environment. If tool support is to be bought, the purchaser should read the chapter in the *Manual,* which gives very strong guidance on the characteristics of tools for DSDM. Not least of these is usability. For some reason, software tools are often less usable than their counterparts in the business environment – maybe we just like to make things hard for ourselves.

10.6 Key points

- RAD tool support is not just for producing technical products faster.
- Wherever possible, tools should be integrated.
- Tool support is particularly useful in testing, configuration management and the production of documentation.
- Do not buy tools specifically for DSDM until the organisation has achieved a level of maturity in the application of the method.

PART TWO

Case studies

This part contains case studies of eight projects. The case studies were all written by people from the projects under discussion. They are of varying depth of detail and breadth of coverage and represent what the authors feel were important aspects of their projects. Each one demonstrates at least one important aspect of the use of RAD. They all speak for themselves but the next few paragraphs give a flavour of what they contain.

The BT case study is the most comprehensive, describing a project in considerable detail. To my mind, the most interesting part of this case study is the graphs of various metrics that were kept regularly throughout the project. The significance of some of the metrics will require careful inspection of the graphs in relation to the supporting text.

The second case study is a disaster project, which had to bring in external help. It was running very late and had completely lost its focus. The organisation is not named for obvious reasons but they set out to use RAD without any understanding of what it entailed. The mistakes they made provide an excellent lesson in what to avoid and what to do better.

As will be clear by now, the user involvement in a DSDM project is essential to its success. The third case study provides the customer's view of a project carried out by Newell & Budge for Scottish Natural Heritage. The ways that the customers worked with their suppliers and their views on the success of the project are given in this case study.

The introduction of DSDM requires different working practices and the use of consultancy support is often essential. The fourth case study describes the support provided to Irish Permanent, Ireland's largest mortgage lenders, by PGT Consultants. The case study gives details about the sort of JAD workshops that were run, why and when.

Sysdeco carried out a project for the *Boston Globe* in the DSDM early adopter programme. One important aspect in this case study is the use of waterfall and DSDM approaches in the same project and why that was necessary. A second is the different productivity metrics achieved in the two parts of the development.

Sema Group is one of the leading European IT companies, with 9400 employees across Europe and Asia. The use of DSDM by such organisations has increased the credibility of the method. The case study presented here is an early project in which they assessed the fit of the method with their quality management system. Sema Group are now using DSDM on some very large projects.

Concerns are frequently expressed about the perceived limitations on the use of DSDM: i.e. only online, only small systems, only new applications, etc. The next case study describes the use of DSDM in a mixed batch and online system upgrade that Orange developed with assistance from a consultant. This pilot project confirmed that DSDM was indeed usable in a wider variety of applications within Orange.

Last but not least, I have included a RAD project that ran before DSDM was published. It contains some contrasts and comparisons with DSDM. Perhaps the most important message of this case study is that DSDM has elements of the way that good RAD projects have been run for some time.

CHAPTER ELEVEN

A measured DSDM project – BT

This chapter discusses a BT project using version 2 of DSDM. At the time the project was carried out, BT had already used DSDM on a number of projects, and it was seen as a key technique in which people should possess skills and experience. However, it was not enough for BT to use DSDM: in order to understand what DSDM would mean to the people who would be using it, it was also necessary to get a feel for the hard factors, such as times spent on different activities, and soft factors, such as the perception of the team and their levels of stress, throughout the project. One major area of concern was that, although developers thoroughly enjoy working in a RAD environment, they can easily burn out through intensive and prolonged working hours. The metrics collected during this project are very interesting in this area.

The case study is largely as written by Ben Whittle, the project manager. The only editing has been to remove any repetition of detail about DSDM. It would appear from the description that the team structure was not as advocated by DSDM, in that the users seem to be described as customers and were not part of the team. However, the user participation was higher than the case study suggests initially (Friday afternoons only).

11.1　The approach to DSDM

The intention was to run the project by the book (i.e. the *DSDM Manual*) with full facilitation support, using all the key DSDM techniques in order to:

- get experience of DSDM;
- determine what worked and what did not, and why;
- determine what information and experiences could be provided for others in BT and the wider community.

BT interpreted the DSDM philosophy to include:

- timeboxing;
- small team size;
- development team collocated in a 'clean room';

- working solely on one project – which is not normal practice in the unit undertaking this project;
- facilitation from DSDM experts – of which BT has a considerable body;
- no outside distractions (such as phones, other project work);
- lots of customer and user involvement, regular reviews with customers;
- restrictions of leave and training within timeboxed periods;
- use of familiar tools and techniques.

The project manager feels that it is unlikely that anyone would ever be in a situation in which all of these conditions could hold true. *(This is probably because BT's interpretation is rather more restrictive than the DSDM Manual, which does not require clean rooms or complete lack of outside distractions.)* This is what happened on the Asset Broker project:

- Timebox: 9 April to 24 May 1996. The timebox was created artificially with customer agreement giving them seven weeks for a project that was estimated at 12 weeks' duration and would traditionally have taken six months, as people would have been working on other projects.
- A development team of four people (with part-time scribe/manager and DSDM facilitation consultant).
- Collocation; the clean room available to the project was an open plan corral within the unit. This is probably a more realistic situation if DSDM is to become widespread – not every team can have a room to itself.
- The development team did work virtually exclusively on the project, with the very occasional hard-fought hours for reviews of previous projects, the unit open day and some development training courses that were not related to the project.
- Facilitation was provided by the DSDM team within BT.
- The clean room had one telephone, which was used as a hotline to customers. The team members' normal numbers were diverted to the unit clerical team or answering machines. Core hours were agreed as 09.30–11.45 and 12.45–16.15 with a daily wash-up meeting at 16.15. The team answered e-mail outside core hours with only one e-mail with a project ID available to the clean room.
- The customers and users fully supported the development and nearly all visited the development at least once a week. A hot desk was set up within the clean room so that one of the users could collocate when possible.
- Conferences and leave that had already been booked took place, in fact the original estimate of four full-time people ended up as an average of 3.2 people per day, once conferences, training and leave had been taken into account. When you add the 'catch-up' time, this results in a considerable drain on the project.

■ The team used the NEXTSTEP OO development environment, an Oracle database and an intermediate webserver for Oracle and NEXTSTEP called Webrex.

The plan was simple: take seven weeks, a week at the start for the business study and a week at the end for implementation. This left five weeks in the middle in which they had five one-week iteration periods: three one-week functional model iterations and two one-week design and build iterations. The weekly focus meant it was easy to tell customers when to come in and review progress (Friday afternoon), and the team could go home for the weekend knowing that the customer was happy with the progress made in the week. The next week's planning could begin on Monday morning. However, once a few public holidays and open days are thrown into the cocktail, things begin to look less clear, as section 11.3 describes.

11.1.1   Quality and testing

The two key areas of concern for experienced developers when they first encounter DSDM are quality and testing. While it is not appropriate to use the most stringent quality, traceability and testing standards, the team were determined to show that the project could be engineered to a good standard. The development methods would be fit for purpose and of sufficient quality that the use of DSDM would be realistic for a development unit. The project had both electronic and paper systems, each with full indexing and configuration.

Some of the measures taken included:

■ User/customer sign-off of requirements and designs on paper copies of the requirements, which were subsequently stored in the paper filing system.
■ When screens were reviewed, a printout of the screen was made and any customer change requests were recorded on the printout and signed and dated by the customers. When the developer made the change, he countersigned the sheet and it was stored in the configuration file.
■ Configuration management – use of the Devman tool. Code configuration came into effect on the Monday of the second week of the functional model iteration. By the end of the project, approximately 300 versions had been made, with three freezes (these freezes corresponded to the end of phases or iterations where the development had been signed off).
■ Daily wash-up meetings, start of the week planning meetings and end of the week review meetings were all short and focused with action points and decisions noted.
■ The project team included two trained auditors, and the team invited a friendly external audit towards the end of the project to check compliance with the relevant development standards.

Since DSDM has no explicit testing phase, the project wanted to ensure that testing did not get marginalised. One of the key metrics gathered was the amount of time spent in testing and related work (see section 11.3). Testing time and techniques on the project included reviewing screens, writing test scripts based on use cases and screens, code reviews and walkthroughs. The team intended to use the CodeReviewer tool for static code analysis, but problems with installation and time-scales meant that this was not possible within the timebox.

11.1.2 Training and team building

The initial intention was to train the whole team in advance of the development. However, the timebox was scheduled to begin early in a new financial year, and at short notice. As a result, only the project manager went on a DSDM practitioner course, three weeks before the project was due to start. As a result of this course, a two-afternoon (8-hour) session was cobbled together with the facilitator in the week before the timebox started covering the key aspects of DSDM and serving as a project planning exercise.

No specific team-building events were scheduled, although the following events were seen as contributing to developing a team focus.

Prior to the project:

- During the time when the project manager was on the DSDM training course, the team were asked to specify the hardware, software and furniture needed to kit out the clean room and assemble as much of this as possible.
- The two-afternoon DSDM training session was used to get people together to think about and agree the ways that they would work and develop and buy into the initial project plan. Some pressure and criticism of the group on a workshop exercise were used to emphasise the benefits of team working.

During the project:

- The team held regular daily and weekly wash-ups, bringing everyone together to note down the achievements and difficulties of the day.
- The team had a regular supply of fruit (the metric was three bananas and an orange each per day) as well as the occasional doughnut, which all served to bring the team together.
- Two open days were planned and carried out as part of the unit activity. This could have been seen as an overhead on the project, but planning it as a risk, being open to the visitors and getting positive feedback, gave a valuable boost to the team.
- The team gave a talk to the unit halfway through the timebox. Repeating the key ideas and achievements to other people and showing what had

been achieved was a great morale booster as well as helping the relationship with the rest of the unit.

■ On several nights (see section 11.3), the team all agreed to work late into the evening to achieve goals.

At the end of the project:

■ A final review was held with the customers, followed by a project review (see section 11.5) and a meal out (at which the project manager gave out small mementoes and 'survivor certificates').

■ The team's final task together was to restore the clean room to its original condition. This activity occurred on the last day of the timebox, after the delivery to the customers. Packing everything up served as a psychological closure and mourning (prior to the night out), and a means of bringing the project to a full stop and enabling another project within the unit to use the area. An end of term spirit prevailed!

The main thing to emphasise on the team-building front was the need to slaughter all the sacred cows (working practices and habits) and build a common agreement on the way of working, to review this regularly and to adapt to any change that would be of benefit.

11.1.3 Project roles and planning

The team consisted of four full-time people, plus one part-time (2 days per week) in the project manager/customer-facing role. The following roles were agreed for the project:

■ Project manager – external relationships, customer and the unit;
■ Team leader – hour-to-hour management of progress and working environment;
■ Architect – overall system architecture, particularly database;
■ Tools – e.g. configuration, code reviewer;
■ User interface design;
■ NEXTSTEP;
■ HTML and Web expert;
■ Scribe – taking minutes at wash-ups, keeping documents and plans up to date.

The roles were divided across the team thus:

■ Team leader and HTML expert – full-time;
■ Architect and tools – full-time;
■ Architect and NEXTSTEP – full-time;
■ Project manager and scribe – 2 days per week;
■ Facilitator – up to 10 days over 7 weeks.

11.1.4   External relationships – managing critical interactions

Three areas of external relationships were identified by the team and each was managed as a risk.

Customers and users

- Relationships with customers and users were managed on a daily basis.
- Organisation and facilitation of more important meetings, such as the initial workshops and end of phase meetings, were organised and facilitated by the DSDM experts, leaving the team to concentrate on delivery.

The unit

- There was some inertia against the use of manpower in a way that was counter to the current model within the unit, and in the use of scarce developer resources on one project for an intensive period.
- Hardware and peripherals (such as the invaluable printing whiteboard) were an initial area in which a great deal of time and political machination were necessary.
- The team ensured a great deal of effort went into the unit open day and an afternoon presentation to the unit followed up by a perception questionnaire (see section 11.3).
- There were two kinds of people who started to interrupt team progress by 'invading' the DSDM clean room: those who were generally curious and wanted to know what was going on, and those that were 'bloody-minded' and wanted to prove that they could come in (both were managed as a risk when the intrusion annoyed the team, but were not evicted as a matter of course, as this may have provoked bad feelings).
- Some team members felt a little pressure from the others in the unit making light remarks along the lines of 'being let out to play'. These were resolved by the team talking through what people felt about the remarks.
- There was an initial feeling among other people in the unit that too much pressure was being put on the team. The open afternoon to the unit did much to dispel these fears.

Other DSDM teams

The DSDM training course and unit open day opened the project's horizons to other teams involved in RAD and DSDM who wanted to see what they were doing and how they were getting along. This informal network of DSDM practitioners met together several times and proved useful for discussing ideas and swapping hints, tips, theories and stories.

The project diary

This section records the major events in the project. The section is not intended to be a full and accurate record, but is for information purposes. The reader may like to consider the events described in this section in order to correlate events to their effects on the team. All of the dates and events are in 1996.

Date	Event
25–27 March	Project manager attends 3-day DSDM practitioner course. Team plan the clean room
1–2 April	Short DSDM course and team project planning (2 afternoons)
9–12 April Feasibility and requirements	9 April – Timebox starts. Meet facilitator to agree workshop agenda, getting the clean room and tools up and running 11 April – DSDM initiation workshop, all customers present
15–19 April Functional prototype First iteration	Goal – First cut of functional prototype screens and develop use cases 16–18 April – Prioritised list of customer requirements completed. Working on use cases with users – lots of meetings. Problems with team pressure – too many small jobs that are not getting us anywhere 19 April – First functional prototype review (prototype) screens
22–26 April Functional prototype Second iteration	Goal – To feed in changes to the screens and develop the functional prototype more. To get a basic object model from the use cases . 23–25 April – Trying to get an object model from the use cases is getting nowhere – we try various approaches but the effect is demotivating, so we abandon it and go straight for the object model – still progressing the functional prototype screens 26 April – Unit open day – much disturbance, but good for morale Second review of prototype screens goes well
29 April – 3 May Functional prototype Third iteration	Goal – To get all of the screens finished for the end of the phase, get agreement on the prioritised requirements and have a good enough object model to proceed with 1 May – Project presentation to the unit – increase in team morale 3 May – Second unit open day – disturbance. Final day of last functional iteration. Prioritised requirements and functional prototype signed off by customers/users
6–10 May Design and build First iteration	Goal – First-cut system to show assets, demonstrating major functionality Steady progress all week. Slower than expected 10 May – Facilitated meeting to agree a new prioritisation with customers that will allow some descoping, if progress continues at this pace

continued over

Customers happy with functionality, some small changes

13–17 May	Goal – To have all the main functions completed
Design and	13–15 May – major machine problems, one development
build	machine dies, with consequent disruption to all and changes
Second	needed to configuration environment – estimated time lost,
iteration	6 person–days
	16 May – Potential problem caused by server 'feature' – decide
	to continue but note a possible post-implementation problem –
	small panic
	17 May – Many late nights this week trying to claw back from the
	lost days earlier in the week and the lack of support from the
	vendors of the server software. Goals not achieved – will have to
	extend into next week – more late nights. Customers happy with
	progress considering problems
20–24 May	Goal – To deliver a fully tested and partially populated system
Implementa-	with trained users
tion	24 May – Project delivery and customer sign-off. Initial post-
	project review, clean up the room and team night out

11.3   Project data

Throughout the development, the team filled in a daily questionnaire. The questions were generated by the team, with the initial idea being for use by ourselves and for other people to review the project. As the project progressed, the graphs were generated and updated and were used within the team for internal management, based on an analysis of the underlying trends. The questionnaire was divided into two parts: the first dealt with the amount of time spent by the team member on different activities; the second with softer factors in the perception of the project progress. The remainder of this section will discuss the results of the study. The team filled in the questionnaire each day after the wash-up or later, if they carried on working. Most of the results in the remainder of this section are averages across all of the full-time people, unless otherwise stated (for example, the total for the whole project includes the time spent by those who were working part-time on the project).

11.3.1   Effort and resource data

Table 11.1 contains the total project data for the development. The upper portion of the table shows the time breakdown for the four developers in the exclusive activities (individual working, etc.) with the subtotals for working with customers and testing. DSDM places a great deal of emphasis on collocation of the team, so the team decided to measure how much time was actually spent working on their own, working together informally, at formal meetings and the time spent on other work that was not part of the project (such as personal development, reading

Table 11.1 Total time spent on the project.

Totals for full-time development staff	Time in hours
Individual work	502.25
Informal networking	220
Formal networking	192.25
External work	112.5
Total DSDM	914.5
Total time	1027
of which, time spent with customers	87.5
of which, time spent testing	223.75
Total DSDM team full-time	914.5
Total customer time	64.5
Facilitator time	26
Manager/scribe	118.5
Total project hours	1123.5

general e-mail, etc.). They found it very useful to measure the time spent on other in order to monitor the amount of total effort that was being put in each day. DSDM encourages a high level of customer contact, so the project decided to measure the time spent with their customers as well. Testing is an area that has no specific phase in DSDM, so they measured testing to see what the testing profile was across the project and to see what proportion of total effort came from testing. Their definition of testing included the time spent reviewing designs and use cases, on code walkthrough, and module testing and developing and implementing test scripts. Lunch times were not included in the summation, but short breaks (up to ten minutes) were included.

Note that the time spent in the different types of working (individual, informal, formal and external) is exclusive, i.e. you can only be working in one way at one time, whereas, for example, you can be informally testing with a customer, giving a value for testing, customer time and informal meetings.

Figure 11.1 shows the total time spent on the different activities for the whole project. Figure 11.2 depicts the average time spent on each task, an average of the collated results recorded by all of the engineers on the given day. Points of interest in Figure 11.2 include:

- a weekly cycle of iterations – effort tends to peak mid-week;
- individual working, informal networking and testing time increase as the project continues: formal meetings are greatest at the start;
- 11 April – project initialisation workshop;
- 16–18 April – use case workshops;
- 26 April and 3 May – unit open days.

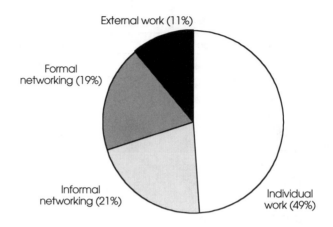

Figure 11.1   Percentage of time in different work styles for full-time DSDM people.

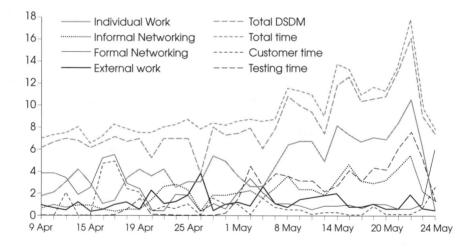

Figure 11.2   Graph of daily effort against time for the average full-time person on the Asset Broker project.

11.3.2   The team's perceptions of the project

The team considered the following questions each day, giving each a score from 1 to 6, with 1 being a disagreement with the statement and 6 being agreement. A 'don't know' (DK) response was also available.

- I am happy with the work in general.
- I feel under pressure.
- I feel stressed.
- I feel excessive disturbance from outside the team.
- I feel good about clean room working.
- The team is working well together.
- The development is going well.
- We will meet our requirements.
- The working environment is comfortable.
- The working environment is conducive to work.
- We are making better progress using RAD than we would normally have done.
- The hardware (including the network) is working well.

Figures 11.3, 11.4 and 11.5 show the trends of these graphs against time. It is probably worth correlating against the project diary in the previous section so that you can see the effect of events (such as the battle with use cases in the week ending 26 April, the unit open days on 26 April and 3 May, or the failure of a machine on 13 May). Note that the stress question was added to the questionnaire on 22 April in order to reflect the team feeling that there was a difference between being stressed and being under pressure.

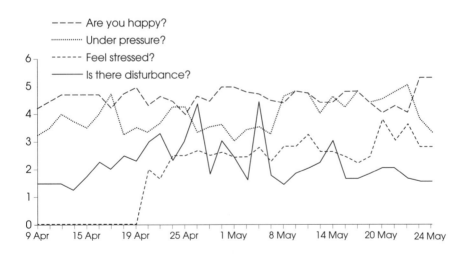

Figure 11.3 Team perceptions of pressure and disturbance during the project, 1 = disagree, 6 = agree.

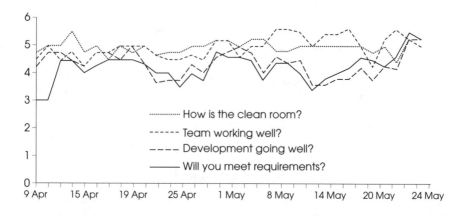

Figure 11.4   Team perceptions of team working and progress during the project, 1 = disagree, 6 = agree.

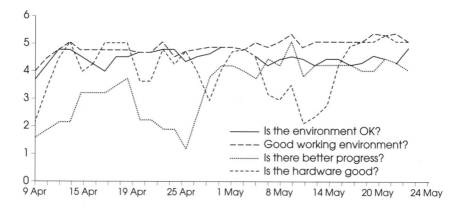

Figure 11.5   Team perceptions of the working environment during the project, 1 = disagree, 6 = agree.

11.3.3   The unit's perception of DSDM and the project

During the fourth week of the project, the team invited the unit to a presentation covering DSDM and the project (approximately 25% of the unit members attended). In the fifth week of the project, unit members were asked to fill in a questionnaire on their perceptions of DSDM and the Asset Broker project. The meeting and the questionnaire helped the project team towards a number of goals:

- helping the team to understand (and therefore manage) the relationship with the other people and projects in the unit;
- the team felt that awareness of the project would help to break down people's misconceptions about the working regime and purposes;
- it was interesting to see what people thought about DSDM and whether they would be interested in a DSDM project, based on what they had seen of the team's work.

The questionnaire was filled in by 19 people, about 60% of those who could have filled in the questionnaire (Table 11.2). The results were gathered between 8 and 15 May 1996. Questions focused on people's perceptions of RAD and DSDM, with particular emphasis on the current DSDM project. Figure 11.6 and Table 11.3 contain a more detailed breakdown of people's perceptions of the DSDM experiment (i.e. the aim of understanding more about DSDM) and of the working practices in general.

11.4 Conclusions and lessons learnt

This case study was written to add to the current knowledge about DSDM within BT. This is a real project; some things went wrong; they had some bad luck; but they did deliver. Please do not take any of the information in this case study as literal truths for all DSDM projects. They are examples from one team on one project. Being part of a DSDM project is hard work and will not suit all people, some projects or some units; be prepared to adapt everything to suit the needs of the team and play to your strengths.

The key lessons learnt during the project were:

- team buy-in to every decision is vital – the team must own the problems and the solutions;
- make sure that your clean room is complete, including all installations of hardware and software tested for the way in which you intend to use them, before the timebox begins;

Table 11.2   SoftLab perceptions of DSDM.

Question	Yes	No
Are you aware of RAD?	19	0
Are you aware of the Dynamic Systems Development Method?	15	4
Are you aware that there is a DSDM development happening in this unit?	18	1

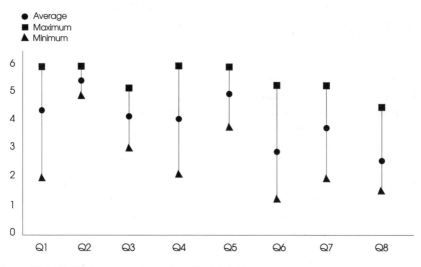

Figure 11.6 SoftLab perceptions of DSDM (detail).

Table 11.3 SoftLab perceptions of DSDM (detailed breakdown)

The questions	Avg	Max	Min	DK	Mode
Q1 Do you understand what the current DSDM experiment is aiming to achieve?	4.36	6	2	0	5
Q2 Is a DSDM experiment the kind of thing BT should be doing?	5.36	6	5	0	5
Q3 Do you feel DSDM is a good way of working?	4.08	5	3	6	4
Q4 Would you like to be involved in a DSDM project?	4.06	6	2	2	3
Q5 Do you think the DSDM development is going well?	4.9	6	4	8	5
Q6 Has the unavailability of the DSDM team caused you problems?	2.53	5	1	0	2
Q7 Do you think the DSDM team is becoming isolated?	3.86	5	2	4	4
Q8 Have you re-evaluated the way you work because of the DSDM ideas?	2.11	4	1	1	1

- make sure up-front that you know who is available when – resource is soon eroded by outside meetings, leave and courses – the team must manage this as a risk;
- small wins – have goals for each week (or perhaps each day) so that progress can be clearly seen (draw a chart on the wall). Recognise small wins, e.g. the doughnut and cream cake bonus at the end of an iteration;

- get customer buy-in to DSDM as well as to the project goals and keep the customers involved with the development – manage their expectations – especially if they cannot make all meetings;
- use and build the contacts with other DSDM projects – you are not alone!

After the project had finished, a project review meeting was held at which more detailed lessons learnt were identified (see the Appendix to this case study, section 11.5). The main thing is that they would all work in a DSDM project again.

11.5 Appendix: Results of the project review meeting

This section records in note form the feedback on the project from the end of project review held on the last day of the project.

11.5.1 What worked well

Results

- system delivered in very short timebox (7 weeks): would not have been possible any other way;
- customers signed off completed system, were pleased with result and impressed by method of working.

Daily wash-ups

- brief and focused (minimum 5 minutes, maximum 30 minutes);
- effective because they were documented (decisions, actions, requirements, etc.);
- continued even when time was short and team not convinced of their usefulness.

Weekly iterations

- reviews of prototypes with customers (Friday afternoons) and team planning meetings (Monday mornings) to set goals for the week.

Clean room

- a 'virtual' clean space (within open plan), worked because it was arranged well (desks in central cluster, adequate personal space, access to walls) and managed well (minimum of interruption from telephones, e-mail, visitors, etc.)

Quality

- ensured by, for example, sign-off of requirements, documented test schedules;

- helped by having auditors in team, plus an invited 'friendly' audit;
- result is a quality product despite the general perception of RAD.

Process

- short timebox and 80:20 rule ensured focus on the real problem;
- external facilitation essential (in this case a DSDM support person plus an independent workshop leader);
- knowledge of the process within the team (in this case project manager was DSDM trained);
- use of dedicated scribe invaluable, especially as it was not a developer;
- management of external interface, e.g. with rest of unit, networking with other DSDM projects;
- measurement of 'soft' metrics added to DSDM process knowledge.

People and teamwork

- team-building helped by project planning exercise combined with the DSDM overview, and by team creating the clean room;
- team all committed to success despite problems and pressures;
- good mix of personalities within team (could not afford any learning time);
- a RAD champion with drive and vision (in this case the project manager);
- core hours and other working practices agreed within the team;
- social events, mutual lunch times, supplies of food, etc. helped team spirit;
- joint working with customers, including some collocation.

11.5.2 What worked less well – lessons, issues, questions

- Planning and baselining: ensure the timebox is big enough at least to get the 'must haves' in (does RAD mean you have to work late into the night to meet the deadline?).
- As far as possible, set up the environment (hardware, software, clean room) before the timebox begins.
- Testing strategy for RAD needs careful planning (e.g. what level of documentation do you need?). The team felt more support was needed from DSDM on testing.
- People work under high pressure in RAD projects – plan recuperation periods following a timebox (e.g. leave, training, wind-down and gradual start-up: not straight into another project).
- Put risk strategies in place, particularly regarding technical skills and hardware (12 days lost to hardware failure).
- Do not assume 100% availability (people's time soon disappears in leave, training, open days, other projects, etc.). Actual utilisation was about 60%.

■ Beware of customer commitment dropping off towards the end. If you are successful, they do not worry and do not think they need to attend – the inverse of what you might expect (possibly an issue of scheduling and diarying customer time up-front).

For more information on this case study, contact Ben Whittle at BT Labs in Martlesham Heath, Suffolk, UK (e-mail bwhittle@srd.bt.co.uk).

CHAPTER TWELVE

How not to do RAD

This case study is necessarily anonymous. It is also much shorter than the detail in the previous one, but it is absolutely packed with things that can go wrong. The case study is from Barry Knowles who was one of the earliest members of the DSDM Consortium and who is one of the many excellent people who contributed their practical knowledge towards the development of version 1 of the method.

12.1 The project

Barry was asked in to manage a RAD project that had gone very wrong indeed – time-scales and estimates had been wildly exceeded and an over-complex design seemed to be impeding progress. His task was to get the project back on track, but a bit of history first...

The project began with an outline specification of the requirements and an estimate for the whole project – three to four years of effort. The next step was to break down the project into functions that could be estimated individually. This resulted in a project estimated at about five years of effort. The project was split into four key functional areas and the four team leaders then dived straight into their respective areas. The only other discussions planned were outline designs and brief descriptions of the online processes and, after delivery, function-by-function user documentation. User participation was not a problem, in fact, if anything, it was too boisterous at times, overpowering the developers with ideas and 'requirements'.

After 18 months and eight years of development effort, there still appeared to be 2.5 years of effort to go.

The company called Barry in. He immediately had the outstanding work re-estimated and made allowances for the various post-programming tasks. It emerged that there were five to seven years of effort outstanding – more than the original estimate for the whole system!

12.2 What had gone wrong?

Almost everything!

RAD had been suggested by their sister company, but there had been no training, and little understanding of the forces that would be unleashed. Neither the IT staff nor the users appreciated what was expected of them in a RAD environment, and although there was enthusiasm and willingness on both sides (certainly initially), the 'team feeling' was missing. The 'them and us' syndrome grew quickly. To make matters worse, some of the users were based on the other side of the Atlantic and, although involved, did not feel part of the development team.

There had been inadequate early planning to get the basic building blocks in place and ensure the development teams were not building on sand – which indeed they were! Early definitions of master files were made without reference to later functionality. Each major functional area was conceived and built with only informal reference to the other areas it interfaced with. Changes would go round in a seemingly never-ending loop, through user to team 1, team 2, team 3 and then back to the user, who perhaps changed his mind again.

There was little focus on organising early deliverables and incremental implementation. In fact, the project deliverables organisation was simply reference files first, followed by master files, online, enquiries, daily batch, reports.

The inadequate documentation of decisions and the lack of formal communication of them resulted in unnecessary revisits to areas already agreed.

There was no timeboxing or controls on functionality being built in. Functionality grew in proportion to the time spent talking about each subject.

There was inadequate overall project management. There was a lead team leader who took overall responsibility for the function but, by the time Barry arrived, she had been put under so much pressure by being the bottleneck through which everything had to flow that she was in grave danger of collapsing under the strain completely.

12.3 So what did he do?

The first task was to reset expectations and then to rebuild confidence in what was achievable with RAD methods.

He reorganised so that responsibility was assigned back to the individual team leaders and he set up coordination procedures. They were able to stem the functionality spread by concentrating on time limits to agree outstanding areas and documenting the agreements, but at the stage the project had reached, it was not so much creeping functionality that was causing slippage. It was the complication that had already been built in, affecting later processes.

They introduced issue-logging procedures, which were prioritised and, thus, responsive to the degree and urgency of the problem, rather than all faults being treated as equally urgent. This enabled them to move more quickly through the testing processes and encouraged the users to assess the business impact of the point they would raise.

The project did not lend itself to the 'test as you go' approach advised by DSDM. This was mostly caused by the sequence in which the system was developed. Unless the project is organised to bring complete processes together at the earliest possible time, testing can only be done at a certain point. In this case, online processes could be tested, but it fell over when a batch process was involved. Batch processes had been left to be developed last.

The problem, however, gave Barry the opportunity to build a new team approach. They identified testing coordinators from the IT and user sides, who would work very closely together. They were empowered to bring in testers and IT personnel as necessary. At every opportunity, he re-emphasised the need, whenever possible, to solve (or at least find solutions to) the problems as they arose – by discussion and increased understanding. Now, finally, the users were seeing the system as theirs, and IT and users understood that they were all part of the same team with the same objectives.

For an outsider coming in, the problems were relatively easy to see, probably less so for those in the swamp surrounded by the proverbial alligators. Even so, it was rather difficult to pick the main lessons from the many that the project learnt. Probably most important and most obvious is that we cannot simply throw away the methods developed over the past 30 years, without having something to replace them with. RAD must not be an excuse for sloppy development practice.

Analysis, careful thought, design and planning are vital to a complex computer system. The temptation to move to a (non-throw-away) prototyping stage too early is great and must be avoided until the business imperatives and approach are clear and a solid overall plan of attack, which is resilient to change, is in place.

Barry's final comment is 'One of the biggest gains is the user buy-in and involvement. Lose that and you are worse off than if you had stuck to traditional methods'.

For more information on this case study, contact Barry Knowles, Dynamic Systems Management Limited (Tel: +44 (0)1727 859050).

CHAPTER THIRTEEN

A customer view – Scottish Natural Heritage

To enable them to manage and allocate funds more effectively, Scottish Natural Heritage undertook to replace its outmoded computing systems. A new system to manage and allocate grants, along with two other projects, was designed and implemented.

There is a line in the *DSDM Manual* saying that the best metric of all is the width of the smile on the user's face. This case study demonstrates just that. Interestingly, the use of DSDM also improved the customer's methods of working in areas outside the project discussed here. The work was carried out by Newell & Budge. The case study clearly demonstrates that collaboration and cooperation can work well with external suppliers – a common concern in purchasing organisations.

13.1 The project

Scottish Natural Heritage (SNH) was established in 1992 under the Natural Heritage (Scotland) Act, with its main purpose being to conserve and enhance the natural heritage of Scotland. It was formed by a merger between the Nature Conservancy Council for Scotland and the Countryside Commission for Scotland.

Scottish Natural Heritage has staff who manage major conservation programmes that include protecting places with high heritage value and preserving rare birdlife and wild animals that inhabit these areas. Projects are as varied as setting up a sanctuary for geese on Islay with the RSPB to organising repairs to footpaths on the Cairngorms.

As a government-funded body with an annual grant of £40m, it has become increasingly important for SNH to manage the funding for the diverse range of conservation activities that it undertakes more efficiently and cost-effectively. A few years ago, SNH realised that its existing computing systems were outdated, unable to support the business requirements that it had and offered little consistency in the way in which the data was stored or used throughout the organisation.

The management team required more accurate information on allocation of funding, projects in progress and staff records and personnel information. In 1994, they developed an IT strategy to help move the business forward, the basis of which was a shared database system.

SNH developed a client/server IT strategy to link up their offices in Scotland and allow staff to access data held centrally and in a consistent format. This formed the basis of the wide area network now in place, which spans its 39 offices. All staff have access to a PC, which is linked by the network to a database server in the Edinburgh office.

This approach has freed up the staff significantly, so time previously spent on administrative tasks is now dedicated to programme work. This work ranges from managing the allocations of money, recording projects carried out to assessing the results achieved, and involves talking to the many landowners, community groups and local authorities and voluntary organisations across Scotland.

A CENTURA database was chosen to hold the central information, such as client records, licence allocations and expiry dates and grant information. The IT strategy highlighted the need to develop client/server user applications that could draw upon data from the database. The front end development tool used for prototyping and development of the production system was CENTURA SQL Windows.

Having established its IT strategy, SNH decided to look at introducing new business systems to enable it to improve the processes that staff use during daily operations. Initially, the company set out with very ambitious targets – to develop six new applications across different functions in less than 12 months. The IT team at SNH knew that the time-scales and the demands were challenging, and this really tested several of the companies who tendered for the business.

Several of the companies that the IT team originally spoke to suggested that it was too ambitious in the targets that had been set. SNH selected Newell & Budge, a systems integration house, who proposed the use of DSDM. The method involved establishing a joint development team with empowered SNH users and project managers working alongside Newell & Budge technical staff to design and develop the systems from the user point of view.

The SNH staff assisted with the design of the user interface, and confirmed typical requests and uses of the system in the working environment. The benefits of this approach were that new systems were up and running very quickly, and were effectively 'designed by the users' so minimising any changes once in place. In addition, the users have a positive approach to using the system, because it does exactly as they specified within the context of their job function.

SNH decided to adopt this approach to develop new applications and set up six project teams. Over a period of just six months, the project teams worked with consultants from Newell & Budge on three of the projects – grant allocation, recording and allocation of licences and a system to record work progress sheets. Kevin Moug of Newell & Budge project managed all three projects. He had overall responsibility for setting up and briefing the teams, which in each case comprised one SNH ambassador user, one team leader and two or more systems builders. The ambassador user in each team was the most senior decision-maker within each department, who had a comprehensive understanding of the business processes and a very clear understanding of the problems and potential solutions. Each team leader was a senior analyst with years of design experience as well as decision-making. The systems builders varied in experience from graduate trainee to seasoned SQL Windows experts.

'It was important that every member of the team understood their role and the level of responsibility which empowerment gave them', said Moug. 'What was fascinating was the speed with which the team established themselves within their roles and worked positively to generate consensus. I remember one early incident, when the ambassador user with years of SNH experience deferred to the advice of a graduate trainee systems builder – albeit after some lively group discussions'.

The team spirit engendered by sharing responsibility for solution finding was reflected in ownership of the end results. SNH was very pleased with the way in which DSDM worked. It brought together the IT department and the user groups who helped to design and develop the systems. The IT department put the application framework in place, while the project manager defined how the system was to be used. For example, development requirements, such as how and when certain forms are used, the training required and critiquing how user-friendly the interfaces are, were all carried out by the project manager.

Weekly checkpoint meetings were held with the IT team to ensure progress against the initial specification and keep budgets and time-scales on track. The tight time-scales meant that a higher proportion than the project manager considered ideal was left to the end users. However, the results of testing clearly indicated that the quality of the systems was not compromised by the pace at which everyone found themselves working.

The DSDM approach worked particularly well with the project team for grants. When a grant application is received, this is logged on to the system and authorised by the administrator. The new system enhances this process considerably, enabling the grants teams to assess the request, authorise and allocate the funds. It also cross-checks whether this request has been received before, or whether money has been allocated before, and flags cases in which an authorisation limit may be exceeded. The grants project manager worked closely with the team from Newell & Budge on the design and development of the user application for the grants department. His role focused on the actual use of the system, which meant ensuring that the system could accommodate the processes involved when allocating funding.

The improved consistency of information and the ability to communicate across different systems has speeded up SNH's processes tremendously. In the case of grants, the whole process is much faster. It shows whether grants have been given and enables SNH to track exactly where funds are being allocated. The built-in flagging of authorisation limits also speeds up the process, highlighting where further action or approval is required by the administrator.

There have also been some other benefits that are not directly tied to the business efficiency. The programme has transformed the way in which SNH now works on projects. Having a project manager involved from the user side means that there is a much greater understanding by the users about what can be done. They have a greater appreciation of the complexity of designing a system and accept more readily the time involved to change what may appear as a simple tweak.

SNH has seen stronger teamwork across different departments, with a better understanding from both sides of what their roles entail. This factor alone has meant that departments talk more readily with each other and work together to solve problems. While being difficult to quantify, these benefits are invaluable to the success of the organisation.

At the end of the project, Newell & Budge held a post-implementation review to understand the lessons learnt from this particular application of DSDM. The positives included:

- Team members found the project much more satisfying than traditional development methods.
- A distinct liking for the empowered team approach resulted in high levels of personal motivation.
- Close involvement with the users resulted in a far greater understanding of the business within which the systems would be applied.
- A high level of satisfaction was derived from problem resolution and demonstration of the solution to the user on the same day that it was identified.

Of the few concerns that were expressed, the main issue was of team selection and dynamics, coupled with the acceptance that DSDM may not be suited to all user representatives or all computer staff.

In summing up the practical issues of delivering client benefits through DSDM, the project manager would emphasise establishing realistic client expectations, particularly in relation to time-scales. As stated earlier, he also placed strong emphasis on each member of the team understanding his or her role in the team. Newell & Budge view this issue as so important that they have now adopted an approach to DSDM project initiation, which involves all members of a team participating in a formal team and roles definition workshop.

Newell & Budge continued to work with SNH to develop the training programmes and assisted SNH in the introduction of the systems. Looking beyond the project described here, SNH sees more opportunities for similar developments. SNH claims that not only were Newell & Budge easy to work with, but they also fostered a close working relationship between the teams. SNH believes that what was done in the time available was a genuine achievement and down to the teamwork and commitment from Newell & Budge and the members of the project team.

For more information, contact Mike Futcher, Newell & Budge, 6 Coates Crescent, Edinburgh EH3 7AL, UK (Tel: +44 (0)131 220 2884).

CHAPTER FOURTEEN

Project support –
PGT Consultants

This case study shows the sort of support that can be useful to organisations that are new to DSDM. It is particularly useful in the detail given about the use of JAD workshops.

14.1 Background

Irish Permanent, Ireland's largest mortgage lenders, had experienced spectacular progress in the non-core business of car financing and life insurance. This saw a 68% increase in its car financing portfolio to Ir£64 million, and life insurance recording earnings of Ir£5.1 million. It was expected that this growth would continue.

In order to service this level of activity, it was decided that the supporting systems needed to be updated and automated. Also, because this growth was happening now and in such significant steps, the time-scale for implementation of the improvements needed to be extremely short.

It was decided by the Irish Permanent IS department that the best way to meet the requirements would be to use rapid application development (RAD) techniques. This was accepted, and a firm of consultants, PGT Consultants, was engaged to assist Irish Permanent in what was for them a totally new way of doing things.

14.2 The project

Irish Permanent have 92 branches throughout Ireland. Their aim is to provide a fast and efficient loan service. Customers are dealt with at the branch and their details downloaded from the host to a PC system. An online application form is completed and a credit check performed. Assuming the credit rating is sound, the terms are agreed and the loan agreed in principle. The loan agreement and the cheque are then printed locally for the customer.

This project proceeded on almost textbook lines from start to finish and PGT Consultants agreed to:

1. Prepare for two JAD workshops and to brief participants.
2. Facilitate two JAD workshops.
3. Advise on the project plan.
4. Conduct periodic project audits with a view to assessing the effectiveness of controls delivered in the project plan and establishing the extent to which the project plan was being followed.
5. Facilitate periodic reviews to monitor progress of the project.
6. Plan, facilitate and report on a post-implementation review of the project.
7. Advise on the JAD workshop progress and RAD critical success factors.

14.3   Briefing for workshop participants

This was carried out in the week before holding the workshop. It covered three main issues: the innovative nature of the project; the importance of communication; and senior management support. The main objectives of the workshop and its agenda were agreed. Finally, a brief synopsis of DSDM and how it was to be applied was given. This ensured that everyone understood the terms being used and how the project was to be organised.

14.4   Initial workshop

This initiation JAD workshop had three objectives:

1. Identify and prioritise functional and non-functional requirements.
2. Produce an outline project plan for the development of the system.
3. Identify key notes likely to impact on this development.

The agenda for the workshop was:

1. Introductions
      a Personal introduction
      b Workshop objectives
      c Agenda overview

2. Scene setting
      a Outline business drivers for this development
      b Why DSDM/RAD?

3. System requirements
      a Identify functional requirements for this system
      b Prioritise functional requirements
      c Identify non-functional requirements

4. Implementation plan for JAD
   a Roles and responsibilities
   b Fit names to roles
   c Identify the main activities (and deliverables)
   d Agree time-scales

5. Risk assessment
   a What are the potential problems and how can they be managed?

6. Issues

The output from the workshop consisted of a high-level project plan (see Figure 14.1), dates when three formal reviews would be held, the size and composition of the DSDM team (see Table 14.1, column 1), a requirements log, which gave a unique reference to baseline requirements, a decision to hold daily wash-up

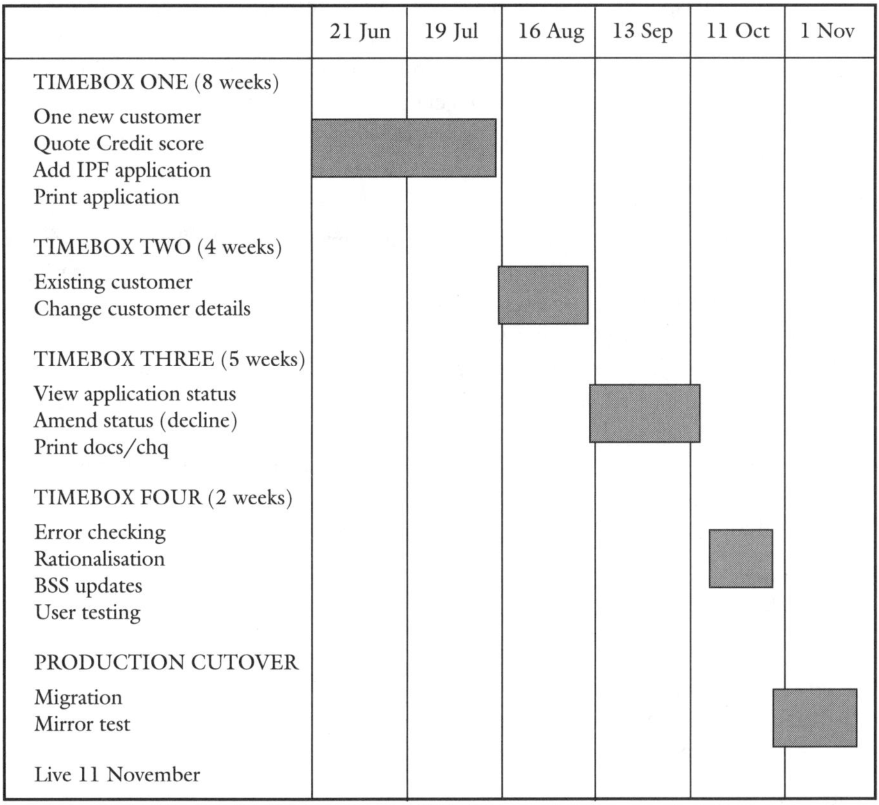

	21 Jun	19 Jul	16 Aug	13 Sep	11 Oct	1 Nov
TIMEBOX ONE (8 weeks)						
One new customer						
Quote Credit score	▓	▓				
Add IPF application						
Print application						
TIMEBOX TWO (4 weeks)						
Existing customer			▓			
Change customer details						
TIMEBOX THREE (5 weeks)						
View application status				▓		
Amend status (decline)						
Print docs/chq						
TIMEBOX FOUR (2 weeks)						
Error checking					▓	
Rationalisation						
BSS updates						
User testing						
PRODUCTION CUTOVER						
Migration						▓
Mirror test						
Live 11 November						

Figure 14.1 High-level project plan.

Table 14.1 Project information.

1 DSDM team	2 Daily wash-up meeting	3 Technology
Two full-time users and numerous adviser users (involved in reviews)	All present 10 minutes –1 hour	MQ Series middleware, UNIX, MVS OS2, Win 95
Team leader from development community	Round the table updates	PC: Visual Age Smalltalk Host: COBOL under
Three PC developers plus eight others	New actions identified	HOGAN umbrella Connectivity: MQ series
Project champion (senior business manager)	Review schedule/ plan	software
Visionary (from business community)	Check new	
Technical coordinator	requirements logged	
Consultancy (PGT and BPR consultant)	Identified benefits and concerns	

meetings (see Table 14.1, column 2) and agreement on the technology to be used (see Table 14.1, column 3).

An important aspect here is the daily wash-up meeting. The time taken for the meeting was variable and dependent on the issues/problems that had arisen that day. It proved extremely valuable in ensuring that problems were highlighted and dealt with quickly and the effect on project progress minimised.

14.5 The project reviews

Three project reviews were conducted with the user community. The objectives of these reviews were to ensure that the business requirements planned for this phase of the development would be met and to demonstrate progress to date. It was important that these reviews were user led.

Once again, the JAD workshop technique was used to ensure speed and efficient decision-making. At these workshops, the requirements were reviewed and the requirements log updated to show the current status and also to ensure that any further requirements were noted and prioritised. The log also indicated whether the requirements had been delivered and demonstrated.

A typical agenda for the project review comprised:

Introduction
    a Workshop objectives
    b Agenda overview

Predemonstration briefing
    a Update on progress to date
    b The purpose of the demonstration

Prototype demonstration
    a Walkthrough of prototype

Prototype review
> a General feedback on the prototype
> b Review of requirements

Issues

14.6	**Summary**

This project completed on time but, at the time of writing, there has been no formal post-implementation review. That is currently being arranged. Nevertheless, there is general consensus within Irish Permanent that the DSDM/RAD has enabled the company to deliver a product in time-scales, which would otherwise have been considered unachievable. The project showed the benefit of having full higher management commitment and the value of access to advice from external sources when taking on new methods and techniques.

The main learning points are as one would expect:

- JAD workshops are a key decision-making technique for DSDM/RAD projects.
- The importance of preparation, particularly for the first workshop, as this sets the scene for the whole development. The work put in by PGT Consultants at this stage, ensuring everyone understood the process and techniques that were going to be introduced, paid dividends later.
- The keeping of a requirements log and ensuring its constant updating made certain that the required business objectives were met and no requirements were overlooked.
- The daily wash-up meetings, which varied from ten minutes to one hour, were key to ensuring that changes and problems were identified early and corrected as quickly as possible.
- Comprehensive functional test plans were produced and kept to.
- The insistence on users leading the demonstrations in the project reviews also acted as a check on understanding of the requirements and ensured that what was finally delivered was usable and held no surprises.

For further information, contact Terry John, PGT Consultants, PO Box 109, Cardiff, Wales CF4 4UT (Tel: +44 (0) 585 746254).

CHAPTER FIFTEEN

An early adopter
case study – Sysdeco

15.1 Introduction

This chapter describes how the *Boston Globe* and Sysdeco (UK) developed a newspaper production tracking system from scratch in four months using the DSDM method, after an attempt to tailor an existing system had failed after 18 months. Sysdeco, being a founder member of the DSDM Consortium, put this project forward for the early adopter programme for version 1 of the DSDM method, for which it was readily accepted. It was from the experiences of this project and others on the early adopter programme that the DSDM method was validated and enhanced in version 2.

What is particularly interesting in this case study is the productivity metrics of the waterfall development versus the DSDM development within the same project with, presumably, the same calibre of people.

15.2 The project

The *Boston Globe*, Boston's major quality newspaper, needed a system to help them manage and track the newspaper production process. They were in the throes of moving away from the old ways of laying out newspaper pages using wax and card, towards full electronic pagination and, as a result, the information required to tell them the production status of the newspaper was now buried deep in computer systems.

The *Globe* had tried to have an existing tracking product tailored to their requirements over a period of 18 months. As this project progressed, it became clear that the system did not, and possibly never would, meet their requirements. This, and the unwillingness of the supplier to consider changing the system, made the *Globe* very uneasy. One of the problems was that the supplier was trying to modify the software without regular consultation with the end users of the system.

It was at this time that the *Boston Globe* turned to Sysdeco to build a tracking system in collaboration with the people who would finally use the system.

The move towards 100% electronic layout and full-page output makes it more important to be able to track the process efficiently in order to meet deadlines. Many people think that all you have to do is have all pages ready by the deadline. To a certain extent, this is true, except that if you can only produce about 30 printing plates per hour (made even worse by the fact that a colour page requires four plates), then only to have all pages ready at the deadline is to fail. The key to success is to achieve an overall page flow. If you have a 120-page issue, then you would aim to have about 20 pages ready per hour, starting six hours before the deadline. You are not concerned with which specific pages are ready, just as long as you have about 20 pages ready for plate production each hour. If you can get some of the pages completed early, you are on to a winner, especially when you consider that it only takes a single element, a headline or a photo caption, for example, to be missing or incomplete to prevent the output of the page. To do this, you need to know the status of any page at any time, and it was important for the *Globe* to access such information quickly and for it to be accurate.

The new tracking system would track the status of each element in the prepress process and warn of evolving problems.

The *Boston Globe* agreed to Sysdeco using a RAD approach to deliver a solution to their production tracking requirements. Sysdeco would use their expertise in RAD projects and their own development tool, Systemator, to deliver the first phase of the system in only four months.

Steve Taylor, executive vice-president of the *Boston Globe,* said at the time 'Sysdeco quickly understood the mission-critical nature of our requirements. Their professional services and Systemator software, which is a key component of the solution, have impressed everyone on the *Boston Globe's* team. Given Sysdeco's prompt and informed response, I feel confident that our project will be a real success'.

The feasibility study started out as an investigation as to why the 18-month tailoring project had failed. It quickly changed to a full feasibility study, once Sysdeco became aware that the only sensible way to go forward was to throw it all away and start from a clean sheet of paper. It is interesting that in this project there was a clear area in which DSDM was not appropriate. The database of status information was to be fed from existing systems, through standard interfaces. The development of these feeds was run as a standard waterfall project. Against the user interface part of the project, Sysdeco applied the suitability filter to the project, and it passed on all counts. This part of the project was a perfect match for a DSDM/RAD approach.

A business study was conducted with the main users in JAD sessions and resulted in the business models (data and process) and overall scope of the project being defined. Misunderstandings of the data definitions were avoided by having them checked by the end users, so that all definitions reflected the business requirement and were fully described in the business terminology of the end users. Also defined was the list of prioritised functions that would drive the subsequent prototyping phases. The involvement of the users at the later stages was also identified. Crucial in this was the ambassador user, who had an overall knowledge of the business areas involved, but also had a good understanding of computer systems. At the end of the business study, an initial prototype was produced to ensure that the general requirements were understood. They also reapplied the suitability filter and tested the project for the critical success factors. Once again, they had a good match on all counts.

The development of the user interface continued in the DSDM framework. A core team of five developers – three Sysdeco and two *Boston Globe* users – commenced the functional prototyping. The whole project was split into two main phases – the first, lasting about four months, to develop a character-based user interface, which would quickly provide the users with the information required, and the second, also lasting about four months, to add graphic 'thumbnail' capability to the system.

The first phase was split into four main prototyping cycles, each delivering a usable piece of the system. The project was such that the design and build of one cycle went in parallel with the functional design of another cycle. The main users, and especially the ambassador user, were integral in the team, commenting on changes to the prototype as they happened. The ambassador user is quoted as saying 'It's a fruitful working relationship. Their people have an office in the building, I meet them every day. They code all day, I test at night. They're prompt in making changes. The give and take attitude really moves things along'.

By June 1995, the character-based system was ready for implementation. This period was also used as a 'cooling-off' period for the team to regain their energy and enthusiasm before going into the graphical-based development. The high level of activity during any RAD project can be very demanding on all team members.

Since the completion of the project, Sysdeco have gathered together the details of how the planning estimates matched the actuals. From an initial look at the figures, it appeared that they had over-estimated the build phase and under-estimated the implementation phase. On closer inspection, they found that this resulted from the effort required to correct problems that only became apparent when they were able to test with real data – once the background data daemon was ready. Their original estimates had allowed for this testing and correcting effort in the build phase, but not the implementation phase. If you incorporate the fix times with the build times and only count the true functional changes in the implementation phase, then the result is actually very close to the estimates. There are the usual swings and roundabouts, with some winners and some losers, but it comes out even in the end.

They also conducted a Mark 2 function point count at the end of the first phase of the project, and the user interface system measured 882 function points. They achieved a productivity of 1.5 hours per function point, which is about 78 function points per man–month. This takes into account the time and effort of all the development team, end users and programmers. The ISBSG median value for all projects is 5.7 hours per function point, which is about 21 function points per man–month. If you look at the data daemon that they were developing in parallel using a waterfall approach, they achieved 5.3 hours per function point, which is about 23 function points per man–month. You can see that the waterfall development of the data daemon delivered a level of productivity at about the ISBSG median, which is about a quarter of the productivity achieved in the user interface system using the DSDM/RAD approach.

In the design of phase 1, the issue of reuse was taken into account, in order to ensure that database handling and filtering routines could be reused for the graphical implementation. The second phase of the overall project was split very much as the first, with prototyping cycles delivering defined parts of the final graphical system. Issues and ideas deferred from the first phase as either out of scope, or where they had been 'dropped' so as to ensure an iteration completion within the timebox, were also incorporated into the final system.

The system is now fully operational, and there are no outstanding functionality issues. The *New York Times*, who now own the *Boston Globe*, have also installed the system. They found it so suitable to their operation that no tailoring was required.

The ultimate proof of a development technique and the success of a project comes not from the programmers but from those who have to use the system. Bob Sylvester, assistant director of information services at the *Boston Globe*, said 'We were impressed by the way Sysdeco approached our problem, and their procedures and tools for developing the new tracking system'.

On any project, it is important for the developers to be highly skilled in the technical environment of the project, but it is equally important for the end users to be highly skilled in the business area, especially in any RAD project. The quality and competence of the end users that were assigned to the project were very important to its success, as only one of the developers knew anything about the production of a newspaper at the start of the project. The willingness of the end users to allow the developers to shadow them in their daily routine enabled the developers to assimilate the business practices involved in the production of the *Boston Globe* quickly. The ability and desire of the end users to answer all of the developers' questions as fully and as accurately as possible to ensure the delivery of the 'right' system is a compliment to their professionalism, and was a major factor in the project's success. They also helped to make it an enjoyable project to work on.

One question is 'Would Sysdeco do anything differently in the future?'. Their answer is that, if they had to repeat the same project today with the same tools and using DSDM, then the answer would be 'No', except for refining their estimating to cater for the lesson they learned, as described a little earlier. Of course, as new techniques, newer and better versions of their tools, become available and when additional versions of DSDM are released, they will adapt their working practices to take advantage of as many appropriate new features and techniques as are available.

For more information on this case study, contact Bob Longman or Ian Smith at Sysdeco in Cambridge, UK.

CHAPTER SIXTEEN

Assessing the quality aspects of DSDM – Sema Group

16.1 Introduction

This system was produced by Sema Group for British Midland. It was an early DSDM project within Sema Group and provided them with assurance that DSDM could fit within a certified quality management system based on ISO 9000.

16.2 Background

16.2.1 British Midland

British Midland is the largest independent UK airline, operating over 1400 flights a week throughout the UK and Europe. British Midland is committed to providing a high standard of customer service and offers its frequent passengers the opportunity to join the airline's frequent flyer programme – 'Diamond Club'.

British Midland is also dedicated to introducing new technology to help provide a better service to its customers. Recently, the airline has pioneered the use of seat booking via the Internet and started trials with smart card ticketing.

Sema Group has provided consultancy and systems integration to BM to support their customer incentive programmes through improving the flexibility of the IT systems. These have included new incentive programmes for frequent flyers and travel agents, a customer's company contact management system, business analysis and feasibility studies for air fare management and an integrated data repository.

16.2.2 Diamond Club redevelopment

Recently, Sema Group was involved in developing a new Diamond Club administration system. Frequent flyers are enrolled as members of the Diamond Club, and the system records information about them, including flight details when the members swipe their plastic cards at check-in desks. Points are awarded for flights, and members can redeem their points for a variety of rewards. There are a variety of card types: with more points, members can be upgraded to card types with additional benefits; they can also be downgraded, if they do not sustain their activity.

Every quarter, the members are sent a statement showing their activities and redemptions. Every quarter, very old activity points expire and cannot be redeemed.

There are partner organisations who participate in incentive schemes with British Midland – other airlines and associated travel suppliers, such as hotel chains. The system accepts activities from members of partner schemes travelling with British Midland, passing them on to the partners for processing, and accepts activities from other partners where British Midland members have used their services.

An important feature of the system is standard and *ad hoc* extracts, labels and mailshots from the system for communication with members. These interface with Microsoft Word and Excel to provide flexible mailshots and management reporting.

The system is a client/server system using the Microsoft Windows GUI environment. The client software is written in MS Access 2.0, and the server software in Micro Focus COBOL with embedded SQL and Oracle 7 PL/SQL. The server database is Oracle system 7.

The business rationale for the project was to respond to the ever-changing requirements of the marketplace. New and innovative marketing incentive schemes are constantly needed to retain customer loyalty, and existing IT systems were too inflexible to support this. Information in the existing system was too difficult to integrate with other IT products for marketing analysis and mailshots. Finally, the third-party system support costs were prohibitive, and BM wanted a development partner who could work within their IT infrastructure to develop a system using industry-standard methods and tools that they could support internally.

The project started in mid-July 1995, and the system was implemented in mid-December 1995.

16.3   How DSDM was applied

Sema Group had previously used a RAD approach at BM that proved successful, but this approach needed more organisation and better definition of processes and products. They chose DSDM for Diamond Club, as it built on the strengths of Sema Group's own experience and provided the necessary framework and product definitions.

The system is largely online, does not have complex algorithms or processing and had insufficiently detailed requirements, which benefited from the DSDM approach.

The project was fixed price in response to a statement of requirements. The Sema Group team used the DSDM lifecycle as follows:

- **Business study**. Business analysis and JAD sessions were conducted to confirm the requirements and, where the requirements were vague, to identify innovative ways to achieve business benefit.
- **Functional model iteration**. To provide a first cut of the working system and determine screen navigation and content. This used timeboxing and prototyping sessions with key users.
- **System design and build iteration**. This used timeboxing techniques and aimed to complete the functional and non-functional aspects of the prototyped system. All functions were tested.
- **Implementation**. This included system testing to integrate the system elements and provide across-system testing of the client and server elements; acceptance testing – BM designed and executed an acceptance test with support from the Sema Group team. Once the system was accepted, data from the old system was converted to the new system, documentation and online help delivered and installation carried out on departmental PCs. The Sema Group team trained the BM trainers, who then trained the users.

16.3.1 User involvement

The Sema Group team consisted of a development team leader, senior developer (who also acted as technical coordinator) and developer.

BM staff included an overall project manager, scribe and liaison for their IT department, executive sponsor and two other key users with in-depth business and administrative knowledge. These BM staff were in the development team part-time and retained their own jobs as well.

The users contributed ideas for the system, how it should look and work. This allowed the development of a system that was, in effect, designed by the user and, therefore, as close to their requirements as possible.

During the project, other Diamond Club personnel were given completed prototypes of the new system to use for evaluation, which helped its final implementation.

16.3.2 Feasibility study

Sema Group became involved in the development process after the BM business analyst for the sales and marketing area had produced an outline statement of requirements.

These were, in essence, the feasibility study for the project. In addition, they had the existing system and a catalogue of real business needs that were not being met.

These gave Sema Group confidence that the new system requirements were feasible, both functionally and technically, and that DSDM could be applied.

16.3.3 Estimating

Sema Group had known and reliable metrics from the previous development project, and these were built into an estimating model for the DSDM lifecycle. The planned duration of the project was six months. In fact, Sema Group also delivered another small system that had suddenly become critically urgent within the overall project timetable.

16.3.4 Business study

The business study took two weeks. JAD sessions were held to get solutions to problems. The business study report contained the Business Area Definition, the System Architecture Definition, the prioritised functions and the Outline Prototyping Plan, and also included database sizing information. The functional requirements were described in more detail and non-functional requirements listed.

Because of the client/server architecture, it was decided to develop the client functions using the DSDM method, and concurrently develop the server functions with a more traditional approach.

16.3.5 Project management

Timeboxing was used to achieve a steady flow of completed and usable products to the user team. Each project phase was preceded by planning and completed with a review and agreement of progress with BM.

Diamond Club was developed as a fixed-price contract. Change requests were used to manage additional requirements that were agreed to be outside the scope of the business study report. The relationship between Sema Group and BM, which has developed over the years, ensured that all changes were agreed amicably.

16.3.6 Functional model iteration

The functional model iteration took about three weeks. The users were heavily involved in defining the content and the navigation of the screens.

The screens were 'created before their eyes', and users were able to understand the way Sema Group carried out the design process. This has the benefit of gaining user acceptance, motivation and confidence.

At the end of the functional model iteration a first-cut working system was released to the users. A dedicated PC was set up for other members of the Diamond Club department to use the system and make comments.

16.3.7 Prototype management

The key users and the scribe were involved in prototyping sessions. The design work quickly moved to the PC screen, so that the users could see more readily how to use the system. This was really appreciated by the user team – they could understand the system as it took shape before them, and it helped them contribute to the design process.

Three development sessions were held in each prototyping cycle. During a development session, each of the decisions was documented and agreed with all parties before the next session.

16.3.8 Testing

There were two approaches to testing:

- For the client application, there was informal testing of the navigation of the functions and the external design (screens and reports) by the developers and the users.
- For the internals of the client functions and all server functions, there was a more formal and traditional unit testing – with a test plan and expected results.

Working systems were released to a dedicated PC in the Diamond Club department, which was available for the other Diamond Club staff to try out the new system and to record their comments. This helped a wider audience to get involved, feel part of the project team and gain system buy-in.

16.3.9 Design and build iteration

The design and build iteration took nine weeks. It concentrated on completing the functional requirements that had been agreed and partially built during the functional model iteration, and on adding the non-functional requirements. The server functions were completed and tested, before integrating them with the tested client functions.

The users were involved with testing the functions as they were completed, and in preparing for the acceptance testing.

The design and build iteration featured timeboxing of related functions, and completing the functions, incorporating comments from the wider user community.

16.3.10 Configuration management

Configuration management was recognised as highly important to the success of the development. So, a version control environment that supported backtracking was used. A team member was assigned to be the single configuration manager who was responsible for the final integration, testing and release, and managed the use of shared code. As far as possible, developers worked on distinct functional areas and managed their own version control.

16.3.11 Quality assurance

Quality was a major factor as they went through the project. The Sema Group quality department was particularly interested in the work and the use of DSDM.

As well as the testing and user walkthroughs mentioned previously, there were also an internal Sema Group technical review and an internal quality audit, which helped to maintain quality and give assurance to British Midland.

The project was also visited by Det Norske Veritas (DnV), Sema Group's ISO 9001 external auditors. This was the first DSDM/RAD project they had had the opportunity to inspect with Sema Group and they were very interested in the development approach.

They concluded:

- 'The DSDM lifecycle used was not seen to be compromising quality in any way';
- 'All project staff interviewed were able to demonstrate a clear understanding of QA principles, the project was able to demonstrate a customer-focused approach to development that was backed up with a well-organised filing system'.

16.3.12 Implementation

The implementation phase was tailored more to the specific needs of British Midland, and the development contract. It lasted five weeks.

Formal system testing was conducted in preparation for the user acceptance test. The system test was based on threads with expected results and included performance testing, volume testing and a trial conversion.

The user acceptance test was a contractual requirement for BM.

16.3.13 The business benefit for BM

The key benefit is a flexible facility for setting incentives for members using 'rules' based on a wide range of criteria. Another benefit is communication with members; this was improved by flexible search mechanisms for finding and using member information, and is fully integrated with Microsoft Office products.

The system was designed to be easy to use. For example, it made maximum use of visual aids and translating complex user selections into plain English. These techniques, and a common look and feel, have reduced training costs and improved the productivity of the users. The Diamond Club administrators can now spend more time with the club members, and less time working the computer system.

16.4   What Sema Group has learned

Getting consistent access to the users was a continuing problem. External factors distracted the users from the project for a period during the design and build iteration, and the final stages of the project were lengthened slightly to bring them up to speed again.

The use of a fixed-price contract can cause some problems in managing the scope of the project. A trusting working relationship is essential to enable these changes to be managed amicably, and either additional iterations/releases planned or functional priorities changed to accommodate the changes.

There was one design problem in the project. One area of the design was completed and agreed without really analysing whether it would resolve all the users' requirements. This proved to be a problem later in acceptance testing, and design changes had to be made.

Sema Group's conclusion is that DSDM works and they are now regularly using the method in a range of software projects. The users like it and they are expecting to be involved in new applications development. The right system was delivered to time and budget.

For more information on this case study, contact Steve Clapham (the project manager) or Michael Gough at Sema Group UK Business Systems, Norcliffe House, Station Road, Wilmslow, Cheshire SK9 1BU, UK (Tel: +44 (0) 1625 531531; fax: +44 (0) 1625 530911; e-mail: Steve.Clapham@mail.sema.co.uk).

CHAPTER SEVENTEEN

Applying DSDM to a batch and online system upgrade – Orange

17.1 Introduction

Any business data you come across in Orange, the UK mobile 'phone operator that has over 10% of the market, has lots of zeros on the end of it. Volumes, wherever you look, are large or enormous. Information technology has a particularly critical role to play, as the business could not function without it. Manual solutions are often just not feasible because of the problems of finding, housing and managing the required staff, let alone bearing their cost. Manual methods would also not be able to provide the high level of customer service that is fundamental to Orange's reputation.

Another characteristic of Orange is the phenomenal rate of change. This is caused by a combination of increasing volumes and new dimensions brought about by diversification. An example is the launch of the Orange visa card with NatWest. There is a constant introduction of innovative ways of doing business to keep ahead of the intense competition in the personal communications industry. The resulting intense time-to-market pressures on the development of IT systems to support the dynamic business environment caused Orange to move towards DSDM by piloting its use on one of its projects. The DSDM pilot system involved automated payments by credit and debit cards.

One of the things that Orange has in common with the rest of industry is the problem of systems development. It has tried different forms of requirements gathering, using traditional approaches, with varying degrees of formality. It is this area of requirements specification that is the greatest problem for Orange because most development projects involve uncharted business territory. This means that there is a lack of working knowledge in aspects of systems under study.

The Orange systems development lifecycle, like most of industry, is a three-stage one, comprising specification, development and testing. The development process, while traditional, is very productive. The corporate HP Unix and Informix environment provides a good technological platform for development at a considerable rate. Although the norm is traditional programming from specifications, this environment is most suitable for iterative development practices.

The testing phase involves standard practice of systems testing and user acceptance. For Orange, as is the case with most of industry, this is usually where the 'fun' begins. All the problems manifest themselves here. They come down to a poor communications process for the determination of business needs. Some of the rework needed as a result of testing is to correct poorly specified functionality. The other type of rework is to create functionality that was missed in the analysis and specification stage. This re-engineering of the system, so late in the day, is familiar to many developers and is a real killer for projects.

Orange's situation is more problematic than most because its systems have to support new business areas and processes with which users are unfamiliar. This factor means that some deficiencies in new systems are not picked up even in the testing phase as users find it difficult to foresee the way the business will operate. In this case, problems manifest themselves in the operational system with even more critical rework consequences.

Having given background on the development and testing phases, the root of the problem is in the analysis and specification stage. This concerns the activities to determine the business requirements and set the course of the development process. The Orange approach is typical of industry with the responsibility of requirements gathering resting on the shoulders of a systems analyst.

You know the story. The analyst identifies the business management and staff concerned and sets up interviews with them. In the process of one-to-one interviews, the analyst formulates 'the solution'. The overall process is lengthy because of the succession of interviews but, moreover, it is a primitive and unsatisfactory way of eliciting business needs. It is based on a single-dimension approach – the views of a user in isolation. The situation demands a three-dimensional approach as depicted in Figure 17.1. The lack of the second dimension, the collective view, means there will be functional gaps and flaws. The third dimension, the future view, is essential where business change is prevalent and the way in which the business will operate needs to be envisaged.

The analyst is experienced and sincere but has little chance of finding the right solution when he or she is taking the central role with users acting as remote satellites. As far as the users are concerned, in this traditional scenario, IT has taken the responsibility for the development of the system. This includes the process that should ensure the required system solution will be provided when it is needed.

The problems are set at this stage with the consequences surfacing to an increasing extent as projects progress and, particularly so, at testing time. It is at this late stage that rework involves orders of magnitude more effort than that of identifying and rectifying problems in the initial analysis process.

The interest in DSDM is in the context of a strategic innovation programme that permeates the whole organisation. The business change that Orange is constantly undergoing creates opportunities. One of these is the positive attitude of staff to explore and adopt new ways of doing things. Orange had been a full mem-

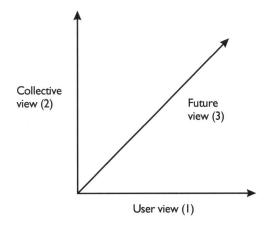

Figure 17.1 The three view dimensions.

ber of the DSDM Consortium for several months before this pilot project and had benefited from the experiences of other DSDM users in the Consortium. These experiences came in the form of papers and via presentations and discussions at regional user group meetings and national conferences.

The bases of the DSDM pilot were to:

- **Select a project that was significant but not business critical**. The project concerned an upgrade to Orange's payments systems to enable the credit card equivalent of direct debit mandates for the automatic payment of monthly accounts. While subscribers can pay automatically by direct debit, a way of doing this by credit or debit card was seen as one of growing interest. The business needed a facility to do this in a five-month time-scale in line with market demand and, in particular, the planned introduction of Orange's visa card, which is co-branded with the National Westminster Bank.
- **See how DSDM could add value to a project that was low on DSDM suitability criteria**. The automated credit card payment system, although online, involved substantial batch processing, including letter production and reports. On the face of it, this provided limited 'prototyping' opportunities, which prevail in DSDM.
- **Use a consultant for advice and guidance**. Someone who had first-hand experience of DSDM-style developments was needed to point the way and facilitate the JAD workshops, which are at the heart of the method. This was seen not as a doing role but one in which Orange would run the project under the guidance of the consultant. He would spend a small amount of time over the project and with the emphasis on the front end activities, so that the project made the right start with firm foundations.

■ **Exploit DSDM within the context of the current development process**. The migration to a new way of working cannot be accomplished in its entirety on the first project. Such a move would constitute too much in the way of risk. The full use of a new approach may not be right and may cause problems that impede the subsequent introduction of it. There are also considerable benefits in using key elements of DSDM.

Ultimately, this pilot project carried the two key objectives of the exercise, that is to:

■ determine the extent to which DSDM could be applied to Orange projects in general;
■ identify the 'cost of ownership', that is the operational changes needed in the business and IT to make DSDM work and whether this provides a net positive contribution.

17.2   Lifecycle/process framework

The three-phase lifecycle used by Orange is presented here in relation to the full DSDM model. Also given here are the key Orange deliverables and the groups constituting the project organisation (Table 17.1). The Orange deliverables are related to DSDM products in section 17.8.

Table 17.1 Lifecycle/process framework.

DSDM process	Feasibility study Business study	Function model iteration Design and build iteration	Implementation
Orange process	Design	Development	Testing
Orange deliverables	Objective business view High-level function definitions System view System components Solution options Prioritised functions Development plan	System component definitions Developed, unit and user tested, iterated system components Operations documentation	System test User acceptance test Technical / operations handover User training
Orange project organisation	JAD workshop group Development team	User control group Development team User/developer teams	User control group Development team User/developer teams

17.3   Orange design process

The philosophy of the design process was to ensure, at the outset, a full objective understanding of the business and all of its high-level functionality in the area under study. This would provide the foundations to determine the extent of computerised support of each of the business functions. From this, the best of the system options, which will support prioritised functions, is decided.

A comprehensive view of the business is vital, irrespective of whether or not business functions would be assisted by computerisation. The business view was represented by a business function diagram. This is a deceptively simple graphical depiction of the overall functional requirements. The technique is described by Crinnion (1991). It is a systematic way of determining and grouping functions that is eminently understandable to business staff. The pilot system comprised seven major functions, which decomposed into 27 subfunctions. Each of the subfunctions was explored and described using a bulleted form of structured text.

Once this objective business view had been elicited, a practical stance was taken on the extent of computerisation and the importance of each of the computerised functions to the needs of the business. The systems options were determined and considered. As with most projects, there is too much to do and too little time. The time-scales are discussed later, but the development phase had an overall six-week timebox. There were sufficient developers to deploy. However, the user involvement in the project brought home the reality of the extent of user resource that would have to go into the project. This was certainly a limiting factor and gave the business management the insight to split the project into two phases.

Of the seven major functions, four were essential to the system and the other three could be accomplished in a later phase. In support of this move, these three other functions were not sufficiently advanced in terms of business knowledge and technical considerations. The project, therefore, focused on four major functions comprising 14 subfunctions.

The next task was to form a systems view. This was extracted from the business function diagram. To achieve this, the systems components are logged with respect to the bullets within each of the subfunctions. Some systems components are common, that is they support a number of subfunction bullets. Some systems components exist already. As a result of this exercise, it was determined that the discrete systems components to be developed were as shown in Table 17.2.

Table 17.2   System components.

Number	System component
2	Screen family
8	Batch process
2	Letter run
14	Report

It should be noted at this stage that the use of techniques in a DSDM project should be determined by the development team. The business function diagram was chosen as the one and only technique. The project involved limited amounts of extra data, such that data modelling would not add value and was not necessary. The users were involved in all aspects of the design process from the objective business view to the identification of the system components. The users had a complete understanding of the project, how it had been created, how it evolved and the functional requirements of the systems components.

With this in mind, the project prepared to enter the six-week development phase. The task ahead, in terms of what was to be developed and the resources required, was discussed and agreed, particularly the commitment of the users. There would be a team leader, four dedicated developers, two dedicated ambassador users and two part-time ambassador users constituting the user/developer teams for the development phase.

17.4   User involvement

The top three priorities for systems development have undertones of Tony Blair's closing speech to the 1996 Labour Party conference. They are user involvement, user involvement and user involvement. This section describes this absolutely vital aspect of DSDM and how users were involved in the workshops, which drove the design process. User involvement in the development and testing phase is described in later sections.

A group of managers and users was identified who represented the relevant business areas:

Orange business area	DSDM role
■ Cash management	Executive sponsor
■ Corporate accounts	Visionary
■ Credit control	Visionary
■ Billing	Visionary
■ Customer services	Visionary
■ Fraud	Visionary
■ Security	Visionary

The managers had no issue with the theory of DSDM, only how to practise it. Their main concern was the buy-in from senior management. This meant that there were really no allowances for the time that managers spend in workshops. They still had their day job and would have to return to duties after a day-long workshop to deal with urgent business matters. Those new to DSDM will have to wrestle with this situation until senior management have changed the culture of the organisation to make development an intrinsic part of the user role.

The pressure that managers were under meant that attending workshops proved a problem. The overall pressures resulted in a somewhat elongated series of workshops as shown in Table 17.3. Two of the managers of the business functions that were less critical to the area under study missed some of the workshops. One of the attendees lacked sufficient seniority and expertise and was not in a position to make decisions in the workshop. In other words, they were not able to exercise empowerment. This was overcome by the project sponsor adopting key aspects of their role by agreement with the manager concerned.

On a number of occasions in the workshops, when there was a potential lack of business expertise, the empowerment issue surfaced. Some voiced the view that this was an empowered group that could make firm decisions on any aspect that arose. This is quite a dangerous aspect of empowerment. The position given by the consultant was that the responsibility of the group was to make 'informed decisions'. The responsibility for decisions was on the group and, if it felt out of its depth in some aspects, such as marketing, then it should seek advice from that area of the business. For the majority of the business area under study, the group constituted all the necessary expertise to make informed decisions. It should be said that sound decisions were made in general, as little backtracking was needed in subsequent workshops.

All of the managers had a significant amount of experience in the business and had been on the receiving end of systems development projects that had gone wrong in the testing phase. They were most enthusiastic about this style of development. However, they expected that their time, which was a most precious commodity, should be used effectively. There were often moments of anguish in the workshops when individual managers were not being used to full effect and

Table 17.3 Workshop activities.

Workshop	Duration (days)	Week no.	Purpose
1	1	1	**Training** – DSDM and the technique to be used **The what** – development of business function diagram (BFD) and subfunctions, i.e. a high-level view of the business area's functional scope and content
2	1	3	**The what** – review and revision of BFD **The what** – development of subfunction bulleted text
3	1	5	**The what** – review and revision of BFD and subfunction text **The how** – discussion of system options **The how** – prioritisation of system functions and phasing **The how** – identification of system components
4	–	6	**The how** – review of system solution **The how** – identification of user involvement in development

thoughts, no doubt, wandered to tasks waiting back in the office. The message of the consultant was to be philosophical and think of the objectives being achieved. Consider the traditional alternative of the analyst conducting one-on-one interviews and how unsatisfactory that process was. Think of the huge ground covered in the workshop. Even if each manager was not fully occupied all of the time, there was a feeling of confidence and satisfaction that the business had been explored in such a thorough manner. This was a most effective way of eliciting requirements.

There was an earlier reference to the unsatisfactory requirements gathering process of an analyst interviewing individual users. This is the one-dimensional view, with reference to Figure 17.1. The workshop group had had first-hand experience of this way and acknowledged that it missed the mark. However, none of the group had previously been involved in a workshop. Despite the pressures, as indicated above, they universally applauded the two other essential dimensions. It added to the requirements eliciting process by providing the collective and future views.

The simple use of a group of experienced business managers provides the collective view. This avoids the functional gaps and omissions that typically result from the one-dimensional interview process. This gathering of managers and the creative, thought-provoking environment also enabled the future view to be obtained. This envisaged how the business would run in a way that was new to everyone. Scenarios reflecting the different user perspectives of the system, both internal and external, unearthed aspects of the system that would otherwise not have surfaced until the system was operational.

Key observations from the workshop activities in Table 17.3 are that the design process was completed in four workshops but that it took six weeks to conduct these. Business commitments and holidays took their toll. Rather than meet sooner with a subset of the group, it was felt by the consultant that a full representation was more important.

It is practical to conduct two workshops per week. This gives just enough time to document each workshop, distribute the material of this and the next workshop, and for the material to be digested by the participants. On this basis, it would have been possible theoretically to conduct the four workshops over two weeks. That would certainly have been rapid. The fact that the duration was long did not, however, detract from the quality of the sessions and the results achieved. So, although the time-scale was not rapid, the process was right.

It was emphasised from the first training sessions that user involvement was absolutely essential throughout The managers constituting the JAD workshop group in the design process would become the user control group in the development process. Here, the group would be responsible for monitoring progress, resolving issues and signing off deliverables. Observations are given in the next section.

The user control group was only required to meet on some three occasions during the development period, as most of the day-to-day work was accomplished by the development team and the user/developer teams. Whereas the workshops occupied a day or half a day, the user control group meetings were one or two hours.

It should be noted that there were logistical challenges throughout the project, as it involved two main sites that are 300 miles apart. Initially, the workshops were based on everyone meeting in the same room. For later workshops and for the user control group meetings, Orange's video-conferencing facilities were used to great effect.

The user involvement in the ensuing development process raised some interesting issues. Most of the business managers could not make the time available to participate in the development role. This is quite acceptable, but on the basis that the manager delegates the role to one of their staff. The responsibility of the manager is to acquaint the person with sufficient background of the project and provide handholding throughout the development period. The term empowerment comes to mind but this describes the practical context of it. The member of staff is acting on behalf of the manager and to be empowered involves initial and ongoing responsibilities on the part of the manager.

The importance of the system to cash management, the manager of which was the executive sponsor, led to the involvement of a senior member of cash management staff as an ambassador user from the outset. This proved invaluable, as the person had an excellent understanding of what was required because of participation in all the workshops. This person was able to be involved full-time in the development process and would call upon a colleague to assist him in the user/developer function.

One of the business managers was able to participate in the development process. This is testimony to her enthusiasm for the DSDM style of working. Having been a key player in the workshops, she had a strong desire to see her work and her system through to fruition.

17.5   Orange development process

Even though the DSDM development process may seem, to first-time readers of the version 2 *DSDM Manual*, to relate only to prototypes, this does not mean only online, screen-based software components. The DSDM approach can and was applied to all software components. These comprised batch processes, letter runs and reports as well as the screen families given in Table 17.2. Of course, batch processes are less amenable to iterative development. But the user can work with the developer to produce them and, once unit tested, they can be provided to the user to test. Indeed, a number of the required reports were directly associated with the batch processes. The definition of the reports and subsequent checking of them in a user-testing exercise complemented the batch process development.

Having commented on the user involvement in DSDM, the role and reactions of the developers is of significant interest. The development team leader was part of the initiative to take on DSDM. In fact, he had attended a one-day DSDM aware course before this initiative and was led to believe that Orange's systems were unlikely candidates for the DSDM approach. Fortunately, that did not dissuade him, and he recognised the potential value of the approach. Four of the senior developers were involved in the workshops and formed, with the team leader, a development group to review the findings of workshops, provide a systems perspective of the exercise and plan subsequent sessions.

There were four developers assigned to the development process and these would be working under the direction of the development team. These four developers were new to DSDM and used to being handed specifications to work from. During a half-day initiation session, the DSDM approach and the background of the project were explained. Then came the point of their role and how they would start on the development process. The developer responsible for a batch process was informed that she should take the subfunction text relating to the batch component and sit down with the appointed user and that they should develop the specification together. Thereafter, she could start coding. This shift in development practice can generate a severe adverse reaction for some. However, in this case, the developer found this new way of operating to be interesting, challenging, refreshingly innovative and effective.

The reaction of all the developers followed this theme and the development work was completed in the planned six-week development period. User involvement focused on working with respective developers on the design of software components. The degree of iteration was limited to the two screen families. For each of the two screen families, a 15-day timebox was used. The batch processes used the DSDM approach in respect of maximising user involvement in design and testing and incorporated other components, that is the reports with which the batch processes related.

The business management who constituted the JAD workshop group continued as the user control group. This group planned to meet three times over the development process duration. In fact, two meetings were organised. It is fair to say that the managers concerned were closely aware of the development work through either themselves or their staff who were working on the project. The purposes of this group were to:

- **Monitor progress**. The development group provided day-to-day control and would raise any progress issues. In fact, progress remained on schedule.
- **Resolve issues**. Again, the development group would handle issues and only take them to the user control group if they were serious. No such issues arose.
- **Accept and sign off delivered components**. Components that had been jointly developed by user/developer teams and user tested within timeboxes would be put to the user control group for acceptance or rework. All components were accepted on first presentation.

A debrief of the development process concluded that it had been completed in a straightforward manner. Moreover, there was a feeling of confidence from the users involved and, therefore, from the developers that the solution was functionally sound. User exposure to and testing of the system had been accomplished well before the system and user acceptance testing phase.

17.6   Orange testing process

System and user acceptance testing is rooted deep in Orange's development practices. The huge volumes processed by Orange's systems, and the severe financial consequences of errors, necessitate such a thorough approach. A four-week period was planned, in line with standards, for system testing and user acceptance testing. While maintaining this extent of testing, the discussion between the consultant and the development team was that this would be an overkill on this project, and subsequent projects could scale down the system and user acceptance testing activity in the light of experience.

In fact, this project was half of a development package. The other half was a technical, performance-related update to the systems. It was planned to combine the testing stage of the two to make a single release. This necessitated the normal testing period as given above and would incorporate system and user testing, and regression testing.

It was interesting to note the reactions of users to this aspect as the project progressed. This was particularly so in the development process in which users were closely involved with design and acceptance testing. Users would ask whether the time-scales of acceptance testing in the final stage should be reduced. This is a most encouraging sign. It provides a good basis on which to make improvements to the application of the DSDM approach to subsequent projects.

A formal iterative process was advocated by the consultant, incorporating the use of testing scripts. The scripts would be produced by each of the user/developer teams in association with the detailed design of the software component. The script would be exercised by the user as the way of testing the software component. This provides a discipline to ensure that testing is thorough and documented for future reference. The recommendations were not fully implemented and, although user involvement was high in the development process, testing was not as thorough as it might otherwise have been.

It should be said that Orange is at odds with the system testing aspect of DSDM, which advocates that this activity should be accomplished incrementally. Orange is of the view that, although incremental unit and subsystem testing of those components of the system being developed is very beneficial, there is always a full system test stage, which will occur at the end of the project. Trying to accomplish full incremental system testing for evolutionary projects on large and complex systems adds unnecessary complexity and resource inefficiencies.

The bonus of DSDM is making the testing process go much more smoothly. Indeed, the reason for trying the DSDM way was to alleviate the panics and re-work subprojects that often feature during the testing process under the traditional development process.

17.7 Conclusions

- **Select a project that is significant but not business critical.** The project was a good candidate. You can wait for a long time for the 'right project' and thereby waste opportunities to get experience from DSDM. Business and technical value was gained and there was little risk to the business in the choice of project.

- **See how DSDM could provide value to a project that is low on DSDM suitability criteria.** Despite the theoretically low rating of this project on DSDM suitability criteria, it was a most suitable candidate. One view of DSDM is that it should be applied to any project that has business value. Such projects should have ownership by the business and that is really what DSDM is about. The extent to which DSDM is applied varies according to the characteristics of the system. Extremes to consider are a totally batch system to a totally online one.

- **Exploit DSDM within the context of the current development process.** Looking at the success of using key elements of DSDM in this project, there will be a review of the DSDM model with respect to the type and scale of all projects. It is likely, however, that the three-phase lifecycle comprising design, development and systems testing processes will remain. A key interest is to shorten design duration by more intensive user involvement. This means an understanding by senior management of the reasons for using DSDM and the effects it has on user resources. There needs to be a real commitment by senior management to this approach, if design durations are to be shortened and if DSDM is to be used in a general way. There is potential for a more formal iterative development process and scripted testing. This would make user involvement more complete. The duration and extent of the testing phase could be reduced because of the testing that has taken place in the development process. The testing phase would focus on system testing. User acceptance testing would be a much reduced activity.

Finally, the two key objectives for this pilot project are discussed.

1. Determination of the extent to which DSDM could be applied to Orange projects in general.

- As a generalisation, it could be said that all projects that have business value should be owned by the business and, therefore, DSDM should be applied. The extent of application depends on the type of project. Even though Orange has its share of 'technical projects', most, if not all, projects have business value. There is, therefore, a wide potential for DSDM.
- DSDM works well and provides substantial benefits on a project that is low on the DSDM suitability criteria. This holds great promise for the application of DSDM on Orange's projects in general.

2. Identification of the 'cost of ownership', that is the changes needed in the business and IT to make DSDM work and whether this provides a net positive contribution.

- This demands a comparison of user resources involved in the traditional and DSDM approaches. Although there is insufficient information, a quantitative view can be taken. The cost of user involvement in the design process is not that much greater than that of the traditional interview process. Although the user involvement in the development process is greater with DSDM, this is balanced against the very high involvement of user resources in the systems and user acceptance testing activities.
- Overall, it is fair to say that there is a higher user involvement with DSDM. How and when users are involved is very much different from the traditional approach.
- The fundamental point is that the DSDM process is far superior. It focuses on the right solution from the start and builds the confidence of all those working on the project.

DSDM worked well on this project. This was achieved by using key elements of DSDM, rather than all of it, and by selecting a system that was low on DSDM suitability criteria. Given that the system is not untypical of Orange's projects, this shows great promise for DSDM in Orange.

17.8	**Appendix**

Table 17.4 is an expansion of Table 17.1 and relates the Orange deliverables to DSDM products. The DSDM products are shown in parentheses below the Orange deliverables. Note that Orange requires a testing phase after development, hence the tested system product occurs in the two phases. The testing phase mainly concerns system testing, as considerable user acceptance testing has taken place in the development phase.

Table 17.4   Comparison of Orange deliverables with DSDM products.

DSDM process	Feasibility study Business study	Function model iteration Design and build iteration	Implementation
Orange process	Design	Development	Testing
Orange deliverables (DSDM products)	Objective business view (Business area definition) High-level function definitions (Business area definitions) System view (System architecture definition) System components (System architecture definitions) Solution options (No equivalent) Prioritised functions (Prioritised functions) Development plan (Outline plan)	System component definitions (Functional model) Developed, unit and user tested, iterated system components (Tested system) Operations documentation (Tested system)	System test (Tested system) User acceptance test (Tested system) Technical/ operations handover (Tested system) User training (Trained users)

For more information on this case study, contact Nick Gill, Olivetti UK Limited, Olivetti House, PO Box 89, 86–88 Upper Richmond Road, London SW15 (E-mail: nick@asis.demon.co.uk).

CHAPTER EIGHTEEN

A pre-DSDM RAD project

18.1 Introduction

This case study is interesting in that it contrasts and compares the approach taken with DSDM. It shows that much of DSDM has been around in RAD for some time, but the conclusion is that, successful as the project was, it could have been run better if DSDM had been around.

18.2 Background

The project involved the development of a system to support the administration of car loans made by a UK county council to qualifying employees. It was undertaken by an external consultant and a senior analyst from the council's IT department. The project sponsor was the head of accounts.

An existing IT system was in use, which had been developed by the previous head of accounts. It had been written using the database facility on the ICL 'One Per Desk' system and had subsequently transferred to a PC platform.

There was a need to make changes to conform with revised regulations for the administration of loans. No documentation had been provided; there was no user manual or any sort of design. The team spent two days analysing the code listings, but were unable to make any sense of them. The program appeared to have been written in a totally unstructured way. They concluded that the system was unmaintainable and that a new system would have to be developed. The fact that the ICL software used in the original development was obsolete and no longer supported gave added weight to this decision.

The IT department had recently invested in development software and a database management system (DBMS) from Oracle. This had been chosen as the standard development software for all projects and so was to be used for the car loans system.

The project was scheduled to take three months, but was subsequently extended by two months. The project was delayed because development took longer than anticipated. Final delivery was then held back because the implementation phase coincided with the end of the financial year, a busy time for both the accounts and IT departments.

They decided to use a RAD/prototyping approach because of the short timescales and because the Oracle system provided them with an excellent prototyping tool.

18.3 Technical environment

Oracle products were used for development – SQL*Forms for online elements, SQL*Plus for offline reports, and the Oracle DBMS for the database. No upper CASE tools were used; they had earlier evaluated Oracle CASE but concluded that it was too expensive to deliver benefits that outweighed the cost. The development platform was an ICL DRS 3000 Unix processor, with PCs at the desktop. The live system ran on an ICL DRS 3000 Unix processor. The users had monochrome text-based terminals connected to the processor via an Ethernet LAN. The team were unable to consider a client/server system because at that time the infrastructure was not available. Similarly, a GUI was not possible either.

18.4 System description

The main functions of the system were:

- enter employee and loan application details;
- record loan approval;
- calculate interest due and monthly payment;
- issue payroll instructions;
- record monthly payment;
- cancel loan;
- update standard interest rate;
- produce loan reports;
- produce summary statistics.

The main data elements were:

- applicant;
- loan;
- current interest rate;
- payment.

Payroll instructions were to be transmitted from the car loans system to a file on the mainframe payroll system. Details of payments made were to be transmitted from payroll to car loans.

18.5 Project planning and organisation

The three-month time-scale was based on an estimate of the time needed for this size of system. This estimate did not prove to be very accurate, and with hindsight was basically educated guesswork, like many project estimates. Estimating was particularly difficult because this was the team's first Oracle/RAD project and the work had to be interleaved with other tasks. They also had to keep the project short to demonstrate that they could deliver results quickly using the newly acquired Oracle technology.

They divided the project into three main phases:

- initial fact-finding, production of a first design and prototype;
- iterative prototyping and further design;
- system delivery and documentation.

They wished to use their standard structured method, SSADM, but needed to tailor this to a RAD approach in order to meet the time-scales. DSDM could not be used because it did not exist at the time.

Their tailoring of SSADM involved selective use of those techniques that could best support the project and replacement of most of the design phase of the method by an iterative prototyping approach. Although they worked out their broad approach to the use of SSADM, they deliberately left things fairly flexible. They felt that they could revisit any elements, if necessary, as the project progressed.

It was decided that the external consultant would develop most of the online elements and the council's analyst would tackle the batch reports. It was not possible to have an end user as part of the team. An Oracle consultant was brought in for five days to assist with a particularly complex element of the system concerning interest calculations. A member of the IT section's network support team assisted with the links between the Unix system and the mainframe and with connecting the users to the LAN.

18.5.1 Compare and contrast with DSDM

1. Tight estimates are important in DSDM projects, but in this case they were not tight enough.
2. The phases of the project did not correspond completely with the DSDM framework. Functional prototyping was not fully separated from design and was spread over the first two phases.
3. The project team did not contain end users.

18.6 End users

The sponsor of the project was the head of accounts. Two members of the accounts staff were to be the main users of the system.

The team recognised from the outset that user involvement in the project was vital, if they were to produce a system to meet their needs. To this end, they took great care to explain the contribution that they would need from them and particularly emphasised that they would need to make significant resources available. The team did their utmost to sell both the project and the benefits of user involvement.

Unfortunately, they only partly succeeded in this. The commitment of the head of department was lukewarm from the start, for reasons that they were never fully to understand. They had hoped that at least two of the accounts staff would participate, but in the event only one of them did so. Despite repeated requests for wider involvement, they were told that the users were too hard-pressed to involve anybody else. A number of the prototyping sessions and meetings that the team arranged were cancelled because there was nobody available to take part. This caused problems throughout the project.

However, the blame for this cannot be laid entirely upon the users. The team felt that they had failed to sell the project sufficiently to the users in order to secure their commitment.

18.6.1 Compare and contrast with DSDM

1. Active end user participation was not fully achieved, but a lot of feedback was obtained from prototyping.
2. Users were not part of the project team.
3. They did not identify the key user roles of visionary, adviser and ambassador.

18.7 Phase 1 – initial fact-finding, first design and prototype

The first step was to talk to the end users to gain an understanding of the problem and an initial set of requirements. This allowed them to start compiling the requirements catalogue and to measure the scope of the proposed system. The team took the opportunity to discuss the level and nature of user involvement in the project with the users and to outline the plans and time-scales.

As the team was using SSADM, the next step was to produce a data flow diagram (DFD) and logical data structure (LDS) for the system. Their tailored RAD approach was to omit the models of the current system and go straight for the required system. Also, they did not decompose the DFD below level one, as this showed sufficient detail to identify the system boundary and the main processes. They intended to use prototyping to define the processing fully later.

The LDS was used to produce a first-cut database, with tables for applicant, loan, payment and current interest rate. This was populated with some 'real' data obtained from the users.

The DFD, combined with the developer's understanding of the required functionality, led to the production of prototype screens for the main functions. This was done fairly quickly and easily, using Oracle SQL*Forms to generate default screens from the database tables and then amending the screen layout.

These were demonstrated to the users to gain some initial feedback, which confirmed that they were on the right lines.

18.7.1 Compare and contrast with DSDM

1. The production of a DFD and LDS conforms with the techniques suggested by DSDM for the business study when using structured systems analysis in the business study phase.
2. They were thinking in terms of tailored SSADM, not DSDM.

18.8 Phase 2 – iterative prototyping, further design

The developers were not sure at this phase how much more SSADM analysis was needed, or possible, given the time-scales. The external consultant produced some initial entity life histories for each of the entities and applied relational data analysis to a number of the screens. There was not enough time to do more than this, so the team were mainly dependent on prototyping for their design.

At this point, it became clear that they were being inconsistent in the layout of the screens. This led to the development of a style guide.

Each function was produced and demonstrated to the users when possible. Most prototypes went two or three iterations. As stated above, the team had trouble getting the users to commit the necessary time and had to make assumptions in a number of places.

The most complex part of the system was the interest calculation module. This had to be based on a complicated standard formula laid down in local government regulations. This would have been relatively straightforward in COBOL, but they had trouble seeing how to do it in Oracle. A consultant assisted with this and succeeded in producing the necessary code. This was tested against a range of manual calculations produced by the users.

Once all the functions were working properly and met user requirements, the team prototyped the menu and help screens. Security requirements, including particular user names, passwords and access controls, were implemented.

18.8.1 Compare and contrast with DSDM

1. Business and usability prototypes were not fully distinguished. They tended to address both issues at once.
2. Timeboxing was not formally applied, although it was by default, because they had limited access to the users.

3. Some non-functional aspects were addressed, e.g. security – not left to a design prototyping phase as in DSDM.

18.9 Phase 3 – delivery and documentation

Testing of individual functions took place throughout development. Each member of the team tested the code that they had developed. Then they passed it to the others for further testing. The final phase involved a test of the complete system to ensure that everything worked together. They also tested performance of the system, which proved to be satisfactory.

A brief user guide was produced, showing all the screens and reports and describing their use. This was not exhaustive in detail, as there were only two or three people in the accounts section who would be using the system. They conducted training sessions for each of the users.

The design documentation and listings were compiled into a system guide as a basis for system maintenance. Procedures were put in place for regular backups of the system by technical support staff. Existing loans were input by the users. This was easier than attempting data conversion from the PC format and the volumes involved were not high.

18.9.1 Compare and contrast with DSDM

1. The end products were the same as the DSDM implementation phase – a delivered system, trained users and a user manual.

18.10 Lessons learnt

- However committed IT professionals are to user involvement in IT projects, it is not necessarily achieved. IT need to work hard to sell the idea and must persist to make it happen. This is one of the advantages of DSDM, with user participation in teams as a key principle.
- Estimating project time-scales as accurately as possible is both vital and extremely difficult. The team wish they had been aware of techniques, such as function point analysis recommended by DSDM, when the project was initiated. They realise that they should have kept records to help them estimate future Oracle projects.
- It may have been better to use iterative delivery of the system functions rather than iterative prototyping and delivery of the whole system. This would have allowed them to deliver something workable earlier and so increased the commitment of the users.
- RAD projects need some sort of framework, as provided by DSDM. Tight controls on the project are, if anything, more important than with large projects. On this project, the team tended to take each day as it came.

18.11 Conclusion

If DSDM had been around, the team would have considered its use, in conjunction with appropriate SSADM techniques. They are also sure that DSDM would have enhanced the success of the project. The other missing element was a powerful, cheap, intuitive CASE tool.

This case study has tended in some areas to focus on the negative aspects of the project to illustrate how it might have been improved by the use of DSDM. It is worth noting that a working system was delivered to the users. The project was a success.

PART THREE

Information

CHAPTER NINETEEN

Where do I go from here?

Contact the DSDM Consortium

The first port of call for more information about the method has to be the DSDM Consortium. The first step to using the method is to obtain the *Manual*. By purchasing the *Manual*, you will automatically become an associate subscriber to the Consortium, which enables you to receive the newsletter, to attend a local user group and to read synopses of white papers as they are produced. To get more detailed information of the method as it progresses and, if you wish, to participate actively in its ongoing development, there are significant benefits to your organisation becoming a full member of the Consortium. Full membership also enables an organisation to attend meetings that are closed to associate subscribers and, at the very least, to have full white papers as they become available from the various work and task groups within the Consortium. These are all the shaded parts of the Consortium structure diagram (Figure 19.1).

The structure of any organisation is critical to its success. It must be flexible, responsive and accountable. The DSDM Consortium structure was created with these three factors in mind: accountable to its members, responsive (rapid) in the development of the method, and flexible in order to adapt to the ever-changing needs of RAD.

Following the transformation of the Consortium into a company limited by guarantee early in 1995, the management committee are in effect the board of directors. They are elected annually by the Consortium members. Each work group is chaired by one of the elected directors.

The technical work group is the 'engine' of the Consortium. It created the DSDM framework and ensures a consistent technical approach throughout the method. Its members all chair task groups that develop and evolve the method. Proposals on the overall direction that the method should take are put together by this group for agreement by the full Consortium. Ideas for method enhancements are also provided by the Consortium membership. At the time of writing, task groups reporting to the technical work group cover topics such as Internet and Intranet development using DSDM, implementing business process change using DSDM, and estimating and metrics.

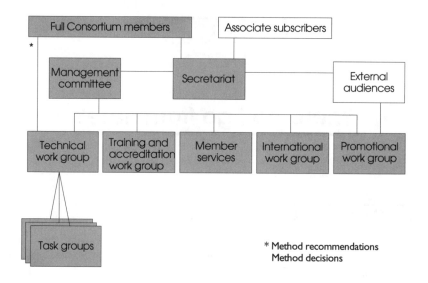

Figure 19.1 Consortium structure.

Participation in work groups and task groups by Consortium members is voluntary. Task group participation can be at one of three levels: low (review only), medium (review and attend task group meetings) and high (where existing and new material is submitted for comment). The mix has turned out to be about right with a few active contributors in each task group and many more reviewers. This has given many members the opportunity to learn from the active contributors, while providing the active groups with comments based on their own practical experiences.

To obtain the Manual *or for further information about the Consortium and its membership, and even how to join, contact the DSDM Secretariat at Kent House, 81 Station Road, Ashford, Kent TN23 1PP, UK (Tel: +44 (0)1233 661003; fax: +44 (0)1233 661004; World Wide Web home page: http://www.dsdm.org; Internet: info@dsdm.org; CompuServe: 100334,1613).*

19.2   Get trained

Because of the major cultural and process changes that come with DSDM, I would strongly recommend that formal training courses are considered. Many organisations offer RAD training, but these can often have a very different flavour from that of DSDM training. Many such courses are focused on using a particular RAD tool. I hope by now that the reader will have found that RAD is far wider in its implications than the use of one or more tools.

There are three forms of training, which are accredited by the Consortium: awareness, practitioner and project management. The Consortium accredits training organisations, individual courses and certifies all trainers. All accredited training is delivered by certified trainers who have been examined by the Consortium at a level higher than that expected of those aiming for DSDM practitioner status.

The awareness training is delivered in one day to all people who have an interest in DSDM. These can be people, such as business managers, IT managers and project managers, who are investigating whether or not DSDM is appropriate to their organisation. The syllabus is general and should be understood by anyone who will potentially be involved in a DSDM project, including users. Indeed, experience shows that an excellent way of kicking off a DSDM project is to have the whole team attend an in-house awareness training course. The result is that everyone understands their respective role and responsibilities within the process.

The practitioner training syllabus is for three days and is aimed at IT staff who will be working in a DSDM environment in whatever capacity. It covers the process and its products, the people and the principles in more detail than is possible in the awareness course.

The two-day project management syllabus assumes that trainees will have attended either an awareness course or a practitioner course. As the name suggests, the focus is on the different approaches to project planning, monitoring and control that come with managing empowered teams and timeboxes. The assumption is that people on the course will know about project management and simply need to learn the different approaches required in a DSDM environment.

Both the practitioner and project management courses contain at least 50% practical work to ensure that the essential ideas covered in the courses are transmitted successfully to the trainees.

Details of accredited training providers are available through the Consortium Secretariat and are on the DSDM web pages.

The DSDM Consortium in the UK runs examinations in the method and issues certificates to successful candidates through the Information Systems Examinations Board, which is part of the British Computer Society. Details of the examination process can be obtained from any of the accredited training providers, from the DSDM Consortium Secretariat or from the DSDM web pages or the Information Systems Examinations Board. Local consortia in other parts of the world start off using these services and move to their own examination and certification processes. Again, the source of information is initially the DSDM Consortium Secretariat in the UK.

19.3   A mentor is essential

When an organisation first considers using DSDM, there are many things that may have to change, even for those organisations who pride themselves on a flexible, mature and controlled process to system development. The impact on the culture within IT and the business areas affected by DSDM projects should not be under-estimated.

It is essential to get the support of someone who has experience of RAD, and DSDM in particular, to make sure that many of the common problems in introducing DSDM are either avoided or managed appropriately. I have tried to cover most of these problems in the text of this book, but the existing culture of an organisation and the personal attitudes of the staff employed in it will make some problems more likely than others.

Until your organisation or someone within it has first-hand experience of DSDM, it is unlikely that everything will go as smoothly as it should. Moreover, it is difficult to believe some of the key messages of DSDM until they have been proven in an organisation. Just telling people from an intellectual point of view will not be persuasive and, worse, may miss some of the important issues.

For instance, one organisation made sure that they had all the infrastructure right for DSDM (including building a special room for JAD sessions) but completely ignored the education of the development team members relating to their special responsibilities within the pilot projects. The only person who knew what the technical coordinator had to do was the technical coordinator himself. It often seemed that they did not know they had a technical coordinator, with the result that all the other developers ignored him. They wasted valuable effort discussing technical issues in which they were not really competent and attempting to make team decisions, which really should have rested with the technical authority on the project.

Many organisations just need a few days' support from a mentor, whereas others need more significant help. The necessary level of mentoring support will depend on each individual organisation. I will not attempt to categorise all the different organisations that I have met in my travels, but here are some of the areas in which a mentor can be very useful:

- 'selling' the concepts of DSDM to senior business management who need to be persuaded that this is probably the best way of getting the system they really need in the time available;
- assessing the suitability of current working practices, procedures and standards to the new approach – this can mean either strengthening weak controls or loosening straitjackets;
- helping to create new working practices, procedures and standards;
- assisting in tool and technique selection;
- assisting the novice DSDM project manager in putting together all aspects of the project plan;
- providing *ad hoc* advice to pilot projects on request;
- visiting pilot projects regularly (say every two weeks) to ensure that they stay on course;
- performing 'health checks' on pilot projects on perhaps a monthly basis.

PART FOUR

Appendix

Documenting the controls

This appendix contains the document used by Logica UK on a project for Shell UK Exploration and Production, called IPSE. It shows many of the aspects discussed in the chapter on timeboxing and is related to Logica's timebox control form shown there. It was specifically defined for that project, but it demonstrates the additional controls that a quality-conscious organisation puts into DSDM.

The project had already delivered several increments and much of the analysis work was complete. There were still design issues to address for the new increment, but the phase would be mostly in the area of software production. The document was produced by an incoming project manager to make explicit the controls that had been in place during the earlier increments.

A.1 Development process

This note aims to clarify the relationship between the IPSE phase IV plan and the individual timeboxes, and to provide an outline process definition for the activities and review points within each timebox during phase IV. This is intended to help ensure that developers and users focus on the correct objectives during each timebox, and that the design coherence of the development is maintained through an effective approach to review and feedback and a clear understanding of what needs to be done at each stage.

At a system level, it is essential to identify and maintain a plan, which ensures that the key business requirements (both functional and non-functional) are addressed and released/delivered in the most appropriate order, and that the availability of resources and ordering of timeboxes match those requirements. At a lower level, it is essential to ensure that each timebox addresses the correct objectives, and that a process is followed which is sufficiently lightweight to avoid being a significant overhead, while at the same time remaining disciplined and rigorous enough to promote acceptable quality levels and overall design cohesion.

The process outlined here is not prescriptive: deviations are perfectly acceptable provided they are justified and alternative means of achieving equivalent quality and design coherence are defined. The process described within each timebox represents a minimum – additional review points or development refinement cycles can be added for any timebox, as agreed appropriate between users and developers.

Section A.2 outlines some major features of the system-level planning and how it interacts with the timeboxes.

Section A.3 details the lower level process within each timebox. Section A.3.1 concentrates on development timeboxes (which are foreseen as consuming the majority of phase IV effort), with an overall process definition and supplementary notes. Possible modifications to the process needed for investigative timeboxes are outlined in section A.3.2.

A.2 System level

As for any implementation project, the phase IV plan needs to identify the objectives, resource allocation, approach, ordering and scheduling of tasks, major risk areas and any major intermediate points and deliveries (e.g. intermediate baselines or major prototype releases). In addition, key elements from a DSDM business study that need to be incorporated are:

- preliminary scoping of the business functions to be supported in timeboxes during the phase;
- definition of the 'type' of each timebox (analytical/development/implementation, etc.) and the categories of prototyping to be performed;
- outlining of which prototypes it is expected to evolve, and which will be discarded;
- identification of the user representatives to support each timebox.

The plan should, thus, identify whether a functional/analytical/investigative timebox is needed before a development timebox in order to achieve any particular set of business objectives, or whether the objectives are understood clearly enough to allow immediate progress to a development timebox. The implementation timeboxes *(Ed: These are detailed design and build timeboxes)*, in which users actively use the software and provide feedback to the developers, and in which the user documentation is completed, also need to be identified and scheduled in the plan.

Any significant horizontal prototyping (e.g. in support of system usability enhancements, end-to-end performance modelling or the integration of major new elements of functionality) needs to be timetabled and resourced.

Timeboxes supporting each major area of business functionality should be grouped in the plan, and allowance made for integration, testing and release to users of each area of functionality as it becomes available.

Where applicable, the plan should also identify specific technical investigative timeboxes to address perceived risk areas (e.g. the PV-Wave interface, where heavy reliance is being placed on the interface; pressure/rate balancing, where one aspect of functionality may be critical to satisfying many businesses; or well modelling, where good performance is critical to system usability).

All of the above need to be in the plan and agreed by the team as early as possible in the phase (ideally, before the timeboxes for the phase are underway).

As the phase progresses and each timebox is performed, the plan will require modification, because the scope of work within each timebox will evolve as the requirements are analysed and prototypes developed. This may affect both downstream and current timeboxes. Checkpoints should, therefore, be built into every timebox, at which the project manager assesses the impact on the overall plan of the work in progress within the timebox and updates the plan accordingly. As a minimum, the process of re-evaluating the plan should be performed after the scoping review, the user key review and the closeout review for each timebox (see section A.3 for details of these review points). At each point at which the plan is re-evaluated to take into account the development activities within a timebox, the progress metrics for the phase should be updated.

A.3 Timebox level

Every timebox, regardless of its type (investigative, implementation, development, etc.), can be considered as comprising three main stages:

1. set up and scoping;
2. development and prototyping;
3. consolidation and closeout.

The main process steps to be followed for each type of timebox are similar, although the names of specific activities and the distribution of effort will vary. Every timebox should feature:

- a high level of user involvement at every stage of the timebox;
- scoping and prioritising of the deliverables according to business needs;
- early feedback/communication of ideas, supported through prototyping;
- a set of defined review points, with specific objectives and roles at each review;
- a key review with an audience (users and developers) wider than the timebox participants;
- evaluation of progress and reconciliation of the timebox activities with the overall objectives for the phase;
- good team awareness of the status of each timebox;
- clearly defined wash-up and closeout process;
- assessment/evaluation of timebox, providing feedback into the plan and the process.

The main steps to be followed for a development-type timebox are identified in section A.3.1, with lower level subsections providing further notes on specific details. Section A.3.2 describes the main variations to the process for investigative/analytical timeboxes.

A.3.1 Development (design) timeboxes

Overall process

The general process for a development timebox can be represented as shown in Figure A.1.

The following list summarises the key elements in the development process within each timebox. By posing each point as a question, it can be used as a checklist to verify that the essential aspects of the process are being addressed.

Set up and scoping stage

1. Prior to starting timebox: define a key user (super-WP-manager) and primary developer who is responsible for implementing the timebox (WP-manager). *(WP = work package, the lowest unit in a Logica project plan.)*
2. Kick-off (KO) meeting (1): hold a timebox kick-off meeting, at which outline requirements for the timebox are defined and prioritised, the schedule, key review points, review roles and criteria and the apparent RADability of the timebox are agreed, the test approach is identified and the need for any additional resources is established (e.g. second developer working within timebox).
3. The type of timebox being undertaken should be clearly agreed between users and developers at the KO meeting. Users and developers should explicitly recognise whether further timeboxes are planned to address the same area of business needs at a later time in the phase.
4. The KO meeting should also agree upon the category of the deliverable software being produced (functional prototype, design prototype, etc.), as this affects the requirement priorities and relative time allocation to

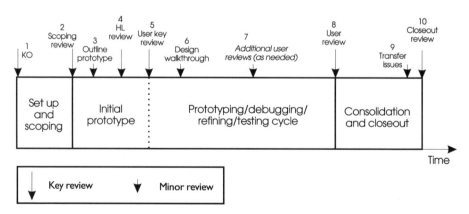

Figure A.1 General process for a development timebox.

different activities within the timebox. At the KO meeting, the technical coordinator should identify any system level issues or actions that represent constraints or requirements on the timebox.

5. Perform a high-level analysis/assessment of the requirements and interaction of the timebox on the existing architecture, produce effort estimates against the prioritised functionality, identify any proposed prototypes and draft a work package completion certificate (WPCC) accordingly. *(The WPCC is the standard document for assigning and controlling work within Logica projects.)*

6. Scoping review meeting (2): hold a timebox scoping meeting, where the initial analysis and developer estimates are used to help refine the requirements, and where the requirement priorities, the essential/optional split, timebox schedule, set of prototypes and review points and the set of deliverable items are agreed between user and developer. The importance of non-functional requirements (maintainability, performance, etc.) needs to be reflected at this stage in the prioritised list of requirements and effort allocation. The need for any specific areas of user support should also be identified. Update the WPCC, which now becomes definitive.

Development/prototyping stage: initial prototyping

7. Outline prototype (3): produce an initial prototype and review it with the user. The essence of the initial prototype is to provide a very early feedback of ideas to the user (e.g. using paper prototypes), in order to stimulate discussion, evolve a better understanding of the requirements and illustrate a range of possible approaches.

8. Clarify the high-level requirements, plus initial ideas on how it is expected they might be met within the context of the existing architecture. Capture this information in the WPDL. *(WPDL = work package daily log, a supplement to the WPCC, which is used in DSDM projects – see section on WPCCs and WPDLs.)*

9. High-level (HL) review (4): review the high-level requirements and design ideas within the development team. The technical coordinator is the key reviewer at this point, but other developers should also participate. Record as action items within the timebox any proposed changes to either the requirements scope or implementation approach.

10. Produce the first-generation prototype.

11. User key review (5): demonstrate/review the first-generation prototype with both the primary user and other users. This is a critical review, at which all users with an interest in the business functions being implemented should attend and provide feedback on the scope and approach. Hold a WPCC review point, at which the WPCC is updated with any agreed revisions to scope. Other issues should be covered by actions.

Development/prototyping stage: prototype refinement and evolution

12. Define the design to a sufficient level to enable the first-generation prototype to be evolved into one which meets the business needs, and record the design in the WPDL. Throughout the timebox, as issues arise and are addressed, they should be documented in the WPDL.
13. Design walkthrough (6): walk through the design with the technical coordinator. Update the WPDL and design as necessary.
14. Perform any necessary updates to the System Architecture Definition and requirements documents (this should be captured from the WPDL by the technical coordinator and incorporated into the system level document). The architecture document should, thus, evolve to capture both the conceptual architecture and the high-level physical software architecture.
15. Perform iterations of second and subsequent phase development within the timebox (refinement and evolution of prototypes, debugging, testing, demonstration and review, etc., as agreed and defined in the WPCC (7). Each iteration is concluded with a user review.
16. Perform testing as agreed in the WPCC.
17. User review (8): hold a final review point/demonstration with the user. No new functionality should be added to the prototype after this point. Agree actions needed to close out the development work for the timebox.

Consolidation/closeout stage

18. Consolidate development by completing actions agreed at user review. Complete testing for the final prototype and update WPDL.
19. Transfer issues (9): agree with the technical coordinator the transfer of any open issues/actions that have been raised within the timebox to a system level issues/actions list.
20. The technical coordinator checks that the System Architecture Definition and requirements documents are up to date regarding the timebox.
21. Closeout review (10): hold a timebox closeout review. Technical coordinator confirms that adequate testing has been performed. Deliverables are checked against WPCC and WPCC is signed off. The user provides feedback on the quality of timebox, which is then attached to WPDL. All timebox issues must be closed (either by being addressed or by agreed transfer to the system level issues/actions list), before the timebox can be completed.
22. If any essential or optional requirements have not been met within the timebox, the decision is taken at this point by the users as to whether a new timebox should be generated to allocate further development effort.

The following subsections provide notes on detailed aspects of the timebox development process.

Scoping of timebox and prioritisation of functionality

If a timebox is to be completed effectively using DSDM, the scope must include a sufficient element of non-essential functionality. It is, therefore, essential for an initial categorisation of business needs into essential and optional to be provided by the user at the KO meeting. The subsequent scoping meeting completes the process of categorisation and prioritisation by taking into account the approximate effort needed to meet each need.

If more than around 75% of the functionality (in terms of implementation effort) is required to meet the essential business needs for the timebox, then the RADability of that timebox needs to be questioned (and revised as appropriate).

Division of effort within timebox

A typical division of effort within a timebox might be approximately:

- 20% set up, scoping and initial prototype;
- 60% design and prototype evolution, debugging and user demonstration/ review;
- 20% consolidation, testing and closeout.

If the nature of the requirements for a timebox is such that the distribution of effort is likely to be markedly different from this (e.g. an investigative timebox or a non-RAD timebox), this should be recognised and clarified at the scoping meeting, and the alternative approach to be taken should be noted in the WPDL.

How many prototypes – at what allocation of effort

The optimum number of prototypes depends on the nature of the timebox. A minimum of two iterations of prototype evolution should be performed (in addition to the outline prototype). This allows the user an opportunity to refine the requirements and tailor the scope of the timebox. The effort being spent on one prototype should typically never exceed around 70% of the prototyping effort.

The effort allocation within the timebox for consolidating the prototype and for testing should not be confused with or budgeted with the prototyping effort.

If less than around 20% of the effort for a timebox is being expended on the consolidation and testing activities, then it should be questioned whether the quality is being unduly compromised.

Deliverables

During the timebox scoping meeting, the planned number of prototype iterations (i.e. interim 'deliveries') and type of prototypes (performance, capability, etc.) should be identified.

Review procedures

Timely review of each work package is essential. There must be a review meeting held at each of the key review points for each timebox. (The quality plan identifies various levels of review meeting.)

The review criteria, the attendees and the roles of each reviewer must be clearly established before the review. This should be done during the timebox set up phase. The quality plan will identify default roles and review criteria.

The technical coordinator provides crucial input to the KO and scoping review meetings, and leads the high-level design review. Ideally, the other developers should also participate in the design review process. The user should lead the KO review, scoping review, user key review, demonstrations and closeout review. All users of business requirements implemented within a timebox should participate in the user key review for that timebox.

Minutes of all review meetings must be taken, and all actions and issues must be recorded in the minutes, with actionee and action date. (The action date must lie within the timebox.) The minutes can subsequently be attached (or referenced) as part of the WPDL. This provides a mechanism for logging and tracking review comments and remedial actions. Actions can only be closed out by agreement of the review leader (typically, the user or technical coordinator), who signs off the action in the meeting minutes to indicate satisfactory completion/closeout.

Integration with other timeboxes

The technical coordinator has a key role in ensuring that the overall architecture is not compromised by the work within any individual timebox, and that the deliverables from each timebox will integrate into the existing system. This role is exercised primarily at the high-level review for each timebox.

Attendance of other developers at the timebox high-level reviews helps to ensure that best use is made of available knowledge, and that all developers retain adequate awareness regarding the design.

Division of effort among timeboxes

As a general rule, at any given time each developer should only be involved in one timebox as the lead developer. It is generally beneficial if the developer also retains some lower level involvement with one or two other current timeboxes (e.g. in a review or support capacity).

Testing

The test strategy for each timebox must be explicitly identified during the timebox KO meeting, and an appropriate effort and time allowance must be made (both by developers and users) to ensure that adequate testing can take place.

One requirement of the WPCC sign-off should be to check that the agreed testing has been performed, and that an adequate record of the testing has been kept. In general, low-level test records will focus on identifying input data (based on equivalence classes) and recording anomalous behaviour as observations. Detailed test designs and test case definitions will not be kept. At a higher level, review minutes following user demonstrations will be used as test records.

WPCCs and WPDLs

The WPCC and WPDL provide the top level definition of objectives, schedule and allocation of responsibility, and the living record of the development process respectively. The WPDL is effectively a working file for the timebox and might, therefore, include extracts from daybooks, relevant notes, design diagrams, etc., plus references to (or copies of) review meeting minutes. If it is not being updated every day during a timebox, then it is not being used properly. As each issue is identified, it should be documented in the WPDL. When the issue is resolved, the WPDL should append the resolution to the definition of the issue.

Documentation

After the high-level review and before closing out each timebox, the system level documentation (the outline requirements list and the architecture definition) should be updated to reflect the development work that has taken place within the timebox. These system level documents remain under the control of the technical coordinator and should be based on material held within the WPDL. Together, these two documents provide a concise, coherent and contemporary overview of what IPSE does and how it does it.

Establishing user support requirements

The users are available to support the development process on request. However, a reasonable attempt should be made by the developer to identify items (files, data, specifications, etc.) that the user needs to provide, and inform the user at the scoping meeting.

Maintaining review records/audit trails

The minutes of review meetings for each timebox are the central means of maintaining review records and providing an audit trail. Each review comment is recorded as an action, which must be signed off by the review leader at a timebox review. All actions must be closed out before a timebox is completed. Actions that cannot be addressed within the context of a timebox must be formally transferred to a system level actions/issues list (under the control of the technical coordinator) to allow closure of the action at the timebox level.

Prototype software should enter into the formal change control mechanism once the timebox in which the software is developed is closed out.

Time recording

The effort expended on each stage of every timebox should be recorded. This supports accounting for the effort spent during the development, and for progress monitoring, and helps to establish any areas of the timeboxes for which effort estimation is regularly inaccurate.

Configuration management

During the development within each timebox, the source code remains under the control of the developer. Upon completion of the timebox, the code is ready for integration into the next incremental release, at which stage it should be placed under more formal change control (i.e. further changes should only be made to address observations, and should be reflected in the file change history).

Abandoning timeboxes

The aim of the development approach is to deliver at the earliest opportunity the functionality that is most important to the business needs. If the business needs or priorities that drive a timebox change, or it becomes clear that a timebox is not going to meet the essential goals, the facility should exist to abandon that timebox. If this decision is made by the users, the timebox should immediately enter a closeout phase. The reasons for abandoning the timebox should be noted in the WPDL and reflected in the procedure for closing out the timebox (i.e. it may not be appropriate to transfer the open issues to system level as part of the closeout for an abandoned timebox).

A.3.2   Investigative/analytical timeboxes

In most respects, the process for investigative/analytical timeboxes is similar to that for development timeboxes. The main points of variation are described below.

- For analytical timeboxes, the level of user involvement is likely to be even higher than for a typical development timebox, as the focus of the effort is on establishing the business needs.
- Typically, investigative or functional analysis timeboxes will be of shorter duration than development timeboxes. This is because much of the analysis for IPSE has already been performed as part of earlier work, and a substantial amount of the software has already been implemented. It is also in line with the DSDM focus on evolving each stage of a process only sufficiently to allow progress to a later stage. The purpose of this type of timebox is to establish requirements only sufficiently to allow them to be taken forward as input to a development timebox, or to investigate a specific technical area in pursuit of a particular objective (e.g. performance analysis as part of a risk management strategy).
- One consequence of the shorter time-scale is that fewer review points may be needed. It may be prudent to combine the high-level review and user key review into a single, user-led meeting. Similarly, it may be appropriate to merge the design walkthrough into a suitable user review. However, note that merging the review points does not remove the need to perform the tasks of each individual review.

- As the focus of an analytical timebox is strongly directed towards establishing the business needs and resulting requirements, it tends to remain at a higher level than a development timebox. As a consequence, there may be a lower emphasis on functioning software prototypes, and a stronger emphasis on paper prototypes and static models.
- The focus of a technical investigative timebox is on a specific issue/range of issues. A relatively higher proportion of effort might, therefore, be expended in establishing a single functioning prototype than with the more iterative, evolutionary approach of a development timebox.

During the course of a development timebox, the objectives of successive prototypes should typically focus in from the initial prototype, which helps to define and evolve the user requirements, to the final prototype, which actually meets the particular business need. In the case of an analytical timebox, the succeeding prototypes may not follow this pattern (e.g. they may explore successively expanding areas of requirements in a breadth-oriented prototype iteration).

Postscript

As in any DSDM development, this book has been written to a very tight time-scale – 20 days' effort with a fixed date for completion of the text.

The executive sponsor was the DSDM management committee who decided that the book was needed and why. The technical work group set the high-level requirements by jointly deciding in a two-hour session what topics to cover. I was the developer who took it through the next stages of the process. The MoSCoW rules were applied throughout, so you may not find your favourite topic, but the essentials are here.

An iterative and incremental approach has been used, obtaining feedback from someone who, although he has many years of experience in IT, had no previous knowledge of DSDM. His comments on both style and content have been useful, but he is only the ambassador user of a very small part of the eventual user population for this book.

I would welcome feedback from the user population as a whole. In particular, if the book is successful and justifies reprinting, I would like to enhance the section containing case studies. If you have a story to tell, please get in touch.

I can be contacted via the DSDM Consortium's postal address, telephone or fax. My e-mail address is *jstapleton@dsdm.org* – probably the preferred method of contact. I look forward to hearing from you.

References

Boehm B. (1986). A spiral model for software development and enhancement. *ACM SIGSOFT Software Engineering Notes*, **11**(4), 14–24. AC, New York

Brooks F. P. (1975). *The Mythical Man–Month*. Addison-Wesley, Reading, MA

Crinnion J. (1991). *Evolutionary Systems Development: a Practical Guide to the Use of Prototyping within a Structured Systems Methodology*. Pitman, London

DSDM (1995). *Dynamic Systems Development Method*, version 2. Tesseract Publishing, Farnham

Gilb T. (1988). *Principles of Software Engineering Management*. Addison-Wesley, Wokingham

Martin J. (1991). *Rapid Application Development*. Macmillan Inc., New York

Rush G. (1985). The fast way to define system requirements. *In Depth, Computerworld*, 7 October

Woodhead R., Atkinson M., Stapleton J., Bray M. and Blackman M. (1997). *Dynamic Systems Development Method and TickIT*. DISC TickIT Office, British Standards Institution, London

Suggestions for further reading

Since the *DSDM Manual* had not been published when these books were written, none of them are totally consistent with DSDM. In particular, the lifecycle is often assumed to be much nearer to the waterfall lifecycle than DSDM would advocate. However, they all contain elements that are useful to the DSDM user.

For an interesting and easy read describing an early RAD project – the successes and the failures:

Kerr J. and Hunter R. (1994). *Inside RAD: How to Build Fully Functional Systems in 90 days or less*. McGraw-Hill, New York

For some very useful checklists and a strong focus on quality in RAD:

Folkes S. and Stubenvoll S. (1992). *Accelerated Systems Development*. Prentice-Hall, Hemel Hempstead

For a view of object-orientated development in a prototyping environment:

Mullin M. (1990). *Rapid Prototyping for Object-Oriented Systems*. Addison-Wesley, Reading, MA

For a view of how structured analysis and design techniques can fit into a prototyping environment see Crinnion J. (1991) – details in reference list above.

And finally, the technology:

Vonk R. (1990). *Prototyping: the Effective Use of CASE Technology*. Prentice-Hall, Hemel Hempstead

Index